flickerbook

an autobiography

flickerbook

an autobiography

Leila Berg

Granta Books

London

First published in Great Britain by Granta Books 1997

Granta Publications Ltd., 2/3 Hanover Yard, London N1 8BE

Copyright © Leila Berg 1997

A CIP catalogue record for this book is available from the British Library

1 3 5 7 9 10 8 6 4 2

ISBN 1–86207–004–0

Typeset by M Rules
Printed by Mackays of Chatham plc, Chatham, Kent

To P. (D)
for his love, for his help,
and for all the things I have learned from him.

Flip-books, or flicker-books . . . a series of sequential pictures or photographs put on separate pieces of paper, one after the other. When the book was flipped quickly through, the pictures would provide the illusion of a moving picture.

Easy-to-make Old-fashioned Toys
Provenzo (Dover)

Contents

The Moon Shines Bright — 1921–1923   *1*

Autumn Leaves — 1923   *11*

People Smudges — 1924   *19*

Killing Jesus — 1924   *28*

Because I Am Seven — 1924–1925   *36*

Moving Staircase — 1925   *45*

The Girl Who Doesn't Know How to Scream — 1925   *54*

The M.D. Class — 1925   *62*

Changing from Minor to Major — 1925   *69*

The Picture Spoke! — 1926–1928   *74*

Tangerine Slices — 1928–1929   *84*

Afraid the World is Falling — 1929–1931   *99*

Plates of Gold — 1931–1932   *113*

Flashes — 1931–1932   *120*

Crying Music — 1931–1932   *125*

England Arise — 1932   *129*

'*Give* me them, *give* me them . . .' — 1932–1933   *137*

'J' — 1933–1934   *146*

Out of Bounds — 1935   *155*

With Grass in her Hair — 1935–1936   *163*

Incantations — 1936   *174*

Tread Softly — 1936   *179*

Words on a Wire — 1936–1937   *191*

Displaced Aristocracy — 1937   *197*

Dreaming of a Song — 1937–1938   *207*

Kissing Fever — 1938   *220*

Waiting in the Dark — 1938–1939   *230*

Some Background Information   *239*

The Moon Shines Bright

1921–1923

I am the Bridesmaid.
I stand on the table.

Sidney's mother is making me a pale-pink frock for Auntie Ettie's wedding. I have to turn round very slowly, while she takes pins out of her mouth like fishbones and squeezes them into my frock.

I must not speak. I must not think. I must not be a nuisance. I must not really be here.

I am turning round very very slowly like the girl on the music-box, standing on the window-sill.

The electric lights tinkle. I hear them like bells.

It is so big, this room. It is called The Assembly Rooms. Not Room. Rooms. Just one room is a *rooms*, because it is so big.

The music sways and curls and dances like the flame of the candle on Friday night. The floor is skiddy, slippery, slidey. I want to sing and shout. I slip my hand into Daddy's, and lean against his knee and look upwards at him. I am so happy. I want to be happy with him.

He snatches his hand away and throws his look at me as if he is throwing a stone. He hates me! My heart stops beating. I am frozen inside. Auntie Ettie says 'Oh look at her! You shouldn't do that to her! She's only three!' Her voice is like a faraway train.

I am hungry. I go and ask Edna for a butty. First she says she is busy, because all the visitors are here. I ask her again. Then she says 'We've got no bread!'

So I go as fast as I can to Mrs Kolnikoff. There are newspapers in the street that wrap themselves round my feet and try to stop me, but I keep kicking them away. The shop is full of people. I try to push between their legs and I get hold of their skirts to pull them so that they let me through. They are like fat trees.

Mrs Kolnikoff can't see me.

At last the shop is empty. Then she sees me. She says 'Hello, pet, what do you want?' and I say 'Bread.' She says 'What kind of bread?' and I point to a really big one, the long kind with seeds. Not the seeds like dashes, but the seeds like dots. She gives it me, and she holds out her hand for the money. But I don't have money, so she says 'When your mamma comes in . . .' And then she says 'Mind you don't fall over, chuck.' She says this because while she is saying it, I am falling. The end of the loaf has got between my feet.

But I get up and take hold of it again, carefully, with my arms right round it. The top end goes into my nose, and the bottom end scratches my ankles and a bit of crust goes into my sock and hurts me when I run again. The newspapers are waiting outside. Some of them are stained yellow. They jump up at my bread like Mr Jernski's dog, as if they want to eat it, but I kick them away. And then Mr Jernski's dog is jumping too, but I don't kick him; I just keep on and on running, because we must have bread.

But all the time the top of the bread is warm against my face, and it is rough outside and warm inside, with a kind smell.

I run into the kitchen. Everyone is there. They are talking to each other. They stop when they see me. I say 'Here's bread,' and I drop it on the floor.

Then someone laughs. And everyone begins to laugh. Everyone, more and more. And their laughing gets further and further away.

I am Bridesmaid again. Standing on the table again, turning slowly. I am four years old. Sidney's mother is making me another frock, for Auntie Sadie's wedding. It is a mauve frock, mauve, a funny sound, like a cow's sound. I like this frock. It is gathered up in little swoops and scoops with little pink rosebuds. Swoops and scoops. A funny sound.

I slide about on the glass floor, swooping and scooping. I don't go near him. I don't touch him at all.

At the bottom of the road and at the top of the road the trams go past. The driver bangs on the bell with his whole hand, clang clang. The sizzling sparking arm of the tramcar reaches up for the wire, like an elephant's trunk searching for bananas. Ellie has a picture of an elephant.

Listen! A motor-car. I look through the window.

A taxi came for Rosie and Louie and their mammy and daddy. Everybody went out to watch. They are going for a holiday, with luggage.

When the taxi had gone away, there was a little puddle of petrol where it had been. And Davey Driberg dipped his toe in the petrol and hopped to a puddle, a water puddle, and put his toe in that. And immediately a rainbow shone out!

I tried to touch the petrol with my toe. But he wouldn't let me. He hit me and kicked me when I tried. But when his mammy calls him in, I do it too. And I make a rainbow puddle of my own.

It's as lovely as the chalk on the pavement, when the chalk is trodden and mixed together by feet. But it's different because it shines.

Who was it *knew* a chair was a chair? Who could tell that was its name? Who could tell that, inside, it had been a chair all the time? And when whoever it was said it out loud, how was it everyone listened, and said 'that's right', and *they* called it a chair too?

On Sunday mornings, Ellie and me wriggle down to the very bottom of our beds, and we stick our heads out of the peronies and talk to each other. The peronies heap up over our heads. They are white snow huts and we are Eskimos. We can lean right out of our peronies and catch fish off the floor and eat it.

We stay in bed late on Sundays, and when we get up we have banana and custard for breakfast.

Is stepstone like stepmother? Stepmothers are in fairytales. Stepstone. It's what you clean the front step with. And then there's hearthstone. And brickstone . . . Evvie and Angie Brickstone . . . It's really Evangeline and Angeline, like princesses' names, but we say Evvie and Angie. Sometimes I think they're called Britstone . . . I'm not sure.

Mrs Miller chases Sidney and Julie round the house with a hairbrush, screaming at them. They run very fast. They are very frightened. I get very frightened too.

Daddy never speaks to me. He is just in the same house.

The croft is black. If you took all the cinders from the fire every morning for years and years and years, and hit them with a hammer till they were very small, you could make a croft. When you fall down on it, your knees bleed, and if you don't have iodine they go green.

Sometimes there are gypsies on the croft in caravans, and they make a fair, and you can go. The horses are white and gold, and they go up and down, and round and round, and the children laugh and their hair blows behind them, and they clutch the poles and they wave and the music plays. I stand by Mammy and we watch. Mammy says watching other people enjoy themselves is as much fun as going on things. Is it?

I wake up in the night, crying. I am very frightened.

I go to Mammy's bedroom, and wake her up so that I can get in her bed. She turns back the cover a bit so I can get in her side. Daddy doesn't move. I stay there a few minutes till I can stop crying and then I go back to my own bed again.

I hate black beetles.

They are all over the floor, and they stop running when you switch on the electric light and freeze, like in *Sly Fox*. You don't see them running because they run in the dark, but when you switch on you know they've been running and it's frightening, because they're so still. You can tell they're holding their breath, waiting for you to switch the light off again.

But it's worst when they are all over the walls, and you might touch one when you switch on the electric light. I hate the way they stand up high on their legs.

Yesterday I was sitting in the wicker chair in the kitchen and I looked at my arm that I'd stretched on the arm of the chair and there was a black beetle walking along my skin. I jumped up and shook my arm over and over again — I couldn't stop shaking it. I would have screamed but I don't know how to.

Last night I had the bad dream again. I keep having it. The little old lady comes down the street and she falls down and she can't get up. She tries, over and over, but she can't. Then she does get up, and she only has one leg.

I got into Mammy's bed for a bit, but I mustn't stay long.

★

You can see pictures on the croft where the gypsies are, but only the boys go there. It's made of wavy iron, the picture house. It clangs like tramcars when boys throw stones at it.

They have Charlie Chaplin pictures. And when it goes wrong the boys throw stones at the pictures, and then the man chases them out. Ellie told me.

> *Oh the moon shines bright on Charlie Chaplin,*
> *His boots are cracking,*
> *For want of blacking,*
> *And his old baggy trousers they want mending,*
> *Before they send him*
> *To the Dardenelles.*

What's Dardenelles? Is that right, 'the Dardenelles'? Nobody will ever tell me. I need to know.

There are two ways to go to sleep. I have my eyes shut, and I look up behind my eyes, as high as I can go, higher and higher, till I hear something click, and my eyes go over the top, and I'm asleep.

The second way is to stroke and rub and twist the place between my legs. It is a beautiful feeling, as if I've come home, like home is in stories. After a while, it goes into a click too, but it takes longer. And then I'm asleep.

Babies have bare bottoms. A lot of children have bare bottoms. Till they go to school, I think. It's to make it easier for grown-ups to slap them.

Zaidie Goller wears a long white cotton shift, like a nightshirt. Like children who have bare bottoms wear out in the street. I don't know what he wears out in the street. I don't know if he goes out in the street. He is a very frum man. Everyone knows that. He is tall, and very thin, and very bony. On Saturday afternoon, a holy time, Mammy and Daddy take me to visit him. They sit in two upright chairs against the wall, and I sit in a third one next to them. Opposite them against the other wall, is a table and a chair. My grandfather sits in this chair, his side facing them, and beckons to me with his long bony finger. They push me to go to him, like a good girl. That is what people always say 'Like a good girl'. He fastens me between his bony legs with his hard sharp knees, pulls down my knickers, and strokes my bottom in a holy way, on and on and on, silently, each Saturday afternoon. Opposite, only a little way off, my Mammy and Daddy watch, silently. I do not feel. I am not there. After a long long time he pulls my knickers up and lets me go, and I go back to my place, next to Mammy and Daddy. This is something you do, if you are a good girl, on Saturday afternoons, which is the time for visiting grandmothers and grandfathers. It's called a mitzvah – that's like 'a blessing'. It blesses him and it blesses me.

Mrs Miller is always screaming at Sidney and Julie and chasing them and hitting them with a big wooden spoon or a hairbrush. When she makes a bridesmaid's frock, she is quite still and quiet.

Down the street there is a very little wooden door. When a grown-up goes through it, they have to bend down. The coalman went through it today. He was bent right down, and I could see over his back. And it was *country* inside – *country*!

It must be a magic door.

Sometimes I go to thread cottons for Bobbie Goller. I have to go past St James's croft.

I don't like the goat. I don't like the tall sunflower either, that jeers over the fence like the boys in the cheder.

I cross the road when I get to the goat, and I cross it when I get to the sunflower, and then I cross back.

*

I think Bobbie Goller is pleased to see me. Otherwise I wouldn't have to go. Would I?

She never speaks to me. She gives me a bobbin of black cotton, and a bobbin of white cotton. And she gives me a packet of needles. I thread needles on to the cotton and they swing there like children on the railings. When she has sewing to do, Mammy says she will take hold of the needle that's on the end and push all the others further on the bobbin, and break off the cotton where she wants.

It is something I am sent to do, because it is a mitzvah. But we don't speak to each other.

Bobbie Goller has still got gas. It goes pop when you light it. It makes me jump, even though I know it will do it. We've got electric now.

Daddy always has his black look. It makes me cold inside.

The sweetshop is called Davidson's. There are Licorice Allsorts in the window, and sticks of Spanish, and licorice laces, and dabs and suckers, and fairy whispers, and luckybags, and gobstoppers. I like luckybags because you don't know what will be in them. They are magic. Once I found a little silver horse inside, wrapped up in white tissue-paper, prancing.

Sidney and Ellie are friends. Then there's Julie – that's Sidney's brother who's a bit younger than me. Julie's hair is cut in a fringe in front, and straight all round. His mother does it with a pudding basin. He's not really my friend, but Sidney is Ellie's friend. We all play Cowboys and Indians over Sidney's wall. Sidney's is a good wall for climbing over, because it's the corner house. Ours is next to it, nearly the corner.

We have a tawse hanging on a nail on the kitchen door. It is for beating children. I don't know if every house has one. I suppose so.

★

I looked through the crack of the little door. I could see the green inside – the *country*. I wanted to stay there a long time, just looking and looking with one eye. But I was afraid another eye might be on the other side, looking at me.

Mrs Rabman is holding her baby up against her shoulder, like mothers do to bring up wind, and patting his bare bottom. She is patting it very fast and laughing, and the baby starts crying, and she says 'Oh, was I patting too hard?', and starts to kiss it instead. Does she do it on purpose?

Today we went to Town for liberty bodices, and in the window of a tiny little shop with diamond windows I saw a *machine* for making toffee. A *machine*. It was like when Mammy puts the skein of wool over my arms and winds it into a ball. The toffee was very pale gold, and it was like silk, shining.

Rapunzel, Rapunzel, let down your hair.

I stood outside the window and watched. I think it goes into those little white and gold boxes that are in the window. They are tied up with gold string. No, thinner than string.
It's a shop for rich people, I think. But anyone can watch.

Bobbie Goller has long hair. I saw it yesterday. I don't know if anyone else has seen it. It is very long and white, like a curtain. I don't know if she saw me. She sits all alone, and combs it.
I think she is not supposed to have long hair. She has that sort of hair like a hat, like all the grandmothers have, and I think that underneath that she is not supposed to have any hair at all. She is supposed to have it all cut off, I think. I don't know why. I don't think she has ringworm. Could all the grandmothers have ringworm?
But this long white hair that she sits combing and combing all alone, her arms going up and down combing and combing, saying

nothing, seeing nothing, just combing and combing – I don't think she is allowed to have it.

Every Saturday morning we all go to shool. I say 'And thou shalt love the Lord thy God, with all thy heart, and with all thy soul, and with all thy might.' Those are all different things.

I had the bad dream again. I keep having it. I had to go to Mammy's bed. This morning Mammy asked me what I keep dreaming about. I said 'It's a little lady. A little lady comes down the street. And she falls down.' I started crying again. Mammy said 'Is that all?' But she can't get up! It is terrible that she falls down and she can't get up!

Daddy beat Ellie with the tawse. Mammy came to get me. She didn't say what she had come to get me for. She just took hold of my hand, and took me. We stood together and I had to watch. She held my hand tight. So that I couldn't run away, I think. But all of me was frozen. I couldn't have run away. He went on and on and on, on Ellie's bare bottom. His face was twisted as if he was trying to do it as hard as he could. With all his might. That is what it means, 'with all your might'.

Ellie's face was so full of trouble and tears. I wanted to scream but I don't know how. I made a quick noise. It came out like a quick laugh. I stopped it at once. Please don't ever let Ellie have heard it, sounding like a laugh, when he was hurting.

And he went on and on. I couldn't move for a long time.

The colours! I shuffle along, not lifting my feet, because I have autumn leaves balanced on my shoes. I am on my way to school. I am five years old.

Autumn Leaves

1923

A terrible thing happens. I fall in the playground right on my tummy, and I can't breathe. I try, and I try. I keep trying to breathe. But I can't. A big girl comes and lifts me up, and she rubs my tummy, and she keeps saying 'It's all right. It's all right. You've only winded yourself.' Winded? I don't know what that is. She keeps on rubbing and rubbing. And I still can't breathe. But at last I can. And I cry terribly because I had forgotten how to breathe, and I am so glad to breathe again.

She takes hold of my hand and takes me inside, and a lady lifts me into a chair and gives me a book to look at. I don't know who she is. I have only just come.

And then the big girl goes away.

I have a doll and pram. Boys have lots of toys, like pistols and caps, and stink bombs, and footballs, and electric things, and cricket bats.

I forgot. I've got a ball, a sorbo one. That's rubber. You can bite it and pull bits off, and it's still a ball, and still bounces, and still looks cheerful, but as if it is covered with crusty sores like Joshy

Reubens. The doll is pot. She has sleeping eyes and real hair. She is very heavy, and very hard. And her knees and elbows and wrists are like a machine. Different layers, so that they bend, but not like a person bends. They bend like something not a person bends.

And the pram has curtains on the hood. I am the only person in our whole street who has a doll and pram like that. Mammy says I should think they're a family heirloom. She says they used to belong to Auntie Ettie when she was little, and I should be proud to have a family heirloom. Nobody else in Fenney Street has a family heirloom. They have old teddies.

I'd really like a teddy. Teddies are soft, and not too heavy to carry, even the big ones. And I could hold it against me and it would be warm. Even one of those baby dolls would be better, that are called celluloid dolls. I know they're hard, really, but they look soft because they're curved, and because they have those little holes – not holes, hollows – in their cheeks and on their hands, and because when they sit down they lean towards you as if they know you'll catch them and hug them. I've seen people and babies do that with each other, and laugh.

And instead of this pram, I'd sooner have an old push-chair, a real one that somebody doesn't want any more, and nobody else needs.

Eta at Number 24 has a teddy, a big one, an old one. It has an empty space near the top like one of Mr Barr's coal-sacks. And one of its ears is ripped, and the cotton hangs down. And one of its eyes is a criss-cross trouser button. And the other one's lost.

I go down to Eta's sometimes, and we change over.

Christian girls don't wear knickers. Knickers are Jewish.

I like *The Big Ship Sails through the Alley-alley-o*, but it's sad somehow. I think it's because it says 'The Last Day of December'. Last days are always sad.

I am playing with Eta's teddy, and her Mammy says I can come inside and have a drink.

I've never been in Eta's house before. We generally play on the step. Eta and me sit together on their black sofa. It is very scratchy and it hurts my legs.

Suddenly – no, not suddenly, slowly; everything goes very slowly like in dreams – there is a big number two next to me on the sofa, hot and smoking like a big sausage. And Eta is standing up on the sofa, leaning against the back and staring at me.

Eta's mother comes in and sees it and says 'Oh Eta, that was naughty' in a soft voice. And she gets a shovel and a brush and takes it away, and gets a wet cloth and wipes the sofa with it, and she says to me 'It's all right now, pet. It's quite clean now,' because she thinks I am quiet because I am worried about sitting there.

But I'm not worried. I'm thinking how wonderful it is, and I want to cry but I'm frozen up inside.

I wish I had a mother who doesn't mind what you do, just lets it happen however it is, and speaks so softly, and lets you be.

We can go into the big bed on Sunday morning. Ellie and I get right under the perony so that no one can see us. We are Eskimos. This morning I was down at the bottom of the bed or maybe the middle, and I started stroking and pressing the place between my legs. After a while Mammy suddenly said loudly, 'What are you doing down there?' so I had to stop and come up. I was hot.

I stand outside when I am by myself, and I press my face against the window, and I watch Mr Davidson breaking up the big slab of Devon Cream toffee. He has a tiny little hammer that kicks up and down like a merry-go-round horse when he bangs the toffee with it. Sometimes he holds a big piece of toffee in his hand and then he bangs down into his hand with a weight from the weighing machine. Both ways it makes a lovely noise. When I grow up I'll have a sweet shop so that I can break Devon Cream toffee, and make that clickety noise. The noise is beautiful. Like a trotting horse. Mr Davidson wears a white coat. He is very clean-looking. So is Ronnie. Ronnie is in my class.

Some mammies say 'wee', but my Mammy says 'Number One'. 'Do you want to do Number One?'

And some people say 'kak', but we say 'Number Two'.

Davidson's is a *good* shop, Mammy says. That is because there is a tray of Devon Cream toffee and a tray of Treacle toffee on the counter. That means the shop is being good. I think mostly because of the Devon Cream toffee. Grown-ups who want a good education buy Devon Cream toffee. They buy it for fourpence a quarter.

Grown-ups' sweet-bags are square like little cushions, and Mr Davidson twirls them round with both hands like when you skip peppers – not like the pointed ones we have for a penn'orth or a ha'porth. Good means whatever makes grown-ups happy.

Christians say Granny. Or they say Nan. They don't say Bobbie. And Christians say Grandad. I have heard Ronnie talking.

I go downhill to school, down the street where the newspapers snarl at my ankles, over the road where the trams charge down like bellowing cows. We went to the country, to Mrs Butterworth's, and Mr Butterworth said 'Those bellowing cows are mad-drunk on windfalls.'

Past the library at the beginning of the park where the three cross librarians hunt down finger-marks, and down the long wide steps. Along the curling paths where ladies and gentlemen made of white stone stand serenely . . . *serenely* . . . in bridesmaids' frocks. They have their names under their feet . . . Juno . . . some of them I can't say, but I have seen those names in books.

Past the flat velvet green where old men will be playing bowls at hometime, (kneeling on silk squares like courtiers in stories). Now comes a magic bit. The iron bridge and the lake. They have come off our three special plates that we keep in a cupboard with windows so that visitors can see them but not touch. How did they come off? How did they get into the park, how did they?

And now through the leaves, the leaves! Crimson and purple and gold! Barred and starred, freckled and speckled, splashed and slashed! Crunching, whispering, scuttling leaves! Is it the leaves I am hearing or the words? Where have they come from, these words?

The ones I pick up I lay on my shoes, and I shuffle along the path, carrying them to school. Every step I see a more beautiful one, and I crouch down again. I put the first one down very gently because I don't want it to be sad that I have left it because there is one more beautiful and more chosen. Then I shuffle on again.

I fill my pockets. Only the tiniest of all for the pocket in my knickers. Put it in carefully, tiny green and red one. I lay more on my shoes, lay some on my shoulders, carry more in my hands, stems tucked into my finger spaces. Autumn leaves!

The library is at the beginning of the park.

You go inside and it is like a little shop, with a counter. The library shopkeepers are behind the counter. There are three of them, a big fierce lady, and two fierce men who are not so big. There is a box on the counter. It has a glass front so that you can see inside it. Inside there are two shelves with some books on them. If I stand on tiptoe I can just see where it shows the name of every book. Grown-ups come in, and they look at the names of the books, and they think for a long time because they are afraid of putting their finger over the wrong book and making the library people angry.

But in the end they have to be brave. They put their finger on the glass so that it sticks up over the top of the book.

15

Then the cross lady and the two cross men can see their finger. But they don't do anything for a long time, because they want to make them wait. Then, if they feel like it, they take out the book, and let the grown-up look at it, to see if he wants to take it home and read it. But he has to make his mind up quickly, or the cross lady or the two cross men will snatch it back and shout at them, because they have no time to waste. There are only the grown-ups and me in the library.

Mammy sends me to get books for her. I have to say 'Mammy says, please can she have a good novel?' The cross lady looks kinder when I say that, and she goes through a little door to get a book for my Mammy. I think she likes choosing a book for people better than people choosing for themselves. I don't think any of the three library people like people choosing one of their books for themselves.

I'm glad I can't reach to put my finger over a book for Mammy. Because as soon as you can do something, you *have* to do it, haven't you?

Bobbie Cohen's eyes are like raisins, or dark-brown gaiter-buttons that you have to do up with a button-hook, and she is always busy and running about. Bobbie Goller is busy too, but not in a running-about way.

I don't see Zaidie Cohen very often. He is generally away, doing his work. He is a watchmaker. When I see him his beard is very tidy like the King's, and not a bit sprawly and floating, or coloured with Russian tea. It is absolutely white. I have seen the King on pennies.

Old men smooth down their floating beards like stroking a cat. Then they put a lump of sugar in their mouth, between their cheek and their teeth. Then they drink the golden tea from the glass. The lemon sails like a moon. And the tea goes through their beard, then it goes through the sugar lump, then it goes through their teeth. I would like to practise it. But the only times we have lump sugar is when the Galanskys or the Cohens come to tea, and you have to reach for it in front of everybody, and they look at you. Bobbie Cohen has little gold earrings like one hair curled round. Bobbie Goller has nothing but her long secret hair.

I practise praying like men pray. I sway backwards and forwards, like the rocking-horse in Lewis's, and I make a singing noise in my nose instead of words that mean something.

He shouts at me. He is surprised as well as angry. Why can't girls pray?

At school, a girl called Florrie sits behind me and pulls my hair. She calls me Carrots and makes faces at me. She is much bigger than me. Her arms are like the legs of the cart-horses, but theirs are lovelier because they are fringed.

Today we had a photograph. We had to come very clean, in our best clothes. Some girls had white pinnies, but I didn't. White pinnies are Christian. I had my mauve crocheted frock. Mammy made me a pale blue one, and a mauve one. I sat on the ground in the front row and Miss Reilly leaned the notice against me. It said 'Grecian Street School, Class 6'. That's the first class. There was a plant in a pot with big leaves next to me, and another one next to Minnie. They were dark leaves. I would never pick up leaves like that, but they're fastened on anyway.

I was glad Florrie was right at the other side. Ronnie was in the back row, standing up. His hair is pale gold like the toffee that winds up in the window. He had on a blazer. Miss Reilly said what it was called. She said 'What a lovely blazer, Ronnie', and touched it. I think blazers must be Christian.

Square bread is Christian. It's called tinned bread. I suppose you get it out with the tin opener. When you cut it, it makes triangles, with sharp neat very beautiful corners.

Jewish bread doesn't have corners. It's round and bulgy, and

17

sometimes it's black, with caraway seeds, and sometimes it's yellow with poppy seeds, and sometimes it's white.

At school we change over for a treat. But I don't tell Mammy. I don't think they tell either.

Chips in shops are Christian chips. Chips at home are Jewish chips. Monty Silver said that there's a Jewish chip-shop called Lazarus opened in Hightown. One day when I'm older I'll go out and find it, like seeking your fortune.

People Smudges

1924

I wrote a poem about the river Thames. That's in London. It ends:

> *I wish I could dive*
> *Ten feet deep.*

I don't really. But that made it rhyme.
I lie on the floor when I write, on my tummy.

Today I wrote about *Bubbles*. That's my comic. It's a tuppenny comic, like *Tiger Tim's*, because it's coloured. The ones that aren't coloured are a penny. It's a poem. It goes:

> *I like toffees and chocolates*
> *And caramels and creams,*
> *But when I have tuppence to spend*
> *Then* Bubbles *is best it seems.*

You have to say toff-EES, and tup-PENCE. And you have to squeeze it up quickly at the end.

19

The reason I wrote about *Bubbles* was that they asked you to. They said 'Write about *Bubbles* and send it to us'. So as I am always writing anyway, I did.

I love the colours of hopscotch when they are scrunched together by feet. Then they go thick and fat and creamy. When they are separate they are thinner.

My poem is in *Bubbles*. I mean, inside it, for everyone to read. They sent me a special box of paper for writing it. The paper is for writing letters. And every piece has all the people in *Bubbles* round the edges. Well, they're not all people. Sometimes they're animals. Bears and tigers.

They didn't say anything about toff-EEs. I don't think it worries them like it does me.

Bobbie Cohen's kitchen is very big. It has red tiles on the floor. It is always full of people, like aunties, but other people too. I don't talk to anyone, but I smile, and sometimes they call me Smiley instead of Leilie.

Edna isn't *exactly* in our family because she isn't Jewish, but she lives with us.

You have to have someone if you're Jewish because you aren't allowed to poke the fire on Shabbos, that's Saturday. At first we only had someone for poking the fire. Then we got Edna.

Bobbie Goller is making ingberlech. You can call them gingers if you like. It is spread all over the big table like a thick tablecloth, but not hanging down. She takes a knife and goes all over the table, criss-cross, criss-cross – hundreds of little golden bricks. She pushes one to me. We don't speak. I just take it.

It is lovely and hot, but not hurting hot. Actually it is quite cold, but it *burns* in my throat.

I have been sent. There is no one else here.

★

Edna stays all the time, not just on Shabbos. Except on her days off, and on Sunday morning when she goes to church. Sometimes on her day off she takes me home with her.

Bobbie Cohen has hens in her back garden. She ties a salt herring to the railing sometimes. She says they like it. It gives them exercise. They get very excited, and they jump into the air, and flap their wings. And they shout in a clinking way like pebbles in a sand-bucket.

Today Mammy sent me to the library to ask for 'a good novel'. There was a man there already, with a cap on. He had brought a book back. The little fierce library man with a moustache was turning over the pages, trying to find a dirty finger-mark or a smudge of HP sauce. It costs a penny for each smudge, whatever it is. If it's Piccalilly, it's bright yellow. HP sauce is brown. Mammy says we don't smudge books in our house. The library man found a very little tear at the edge of one page. Then he turned it over quickly, and said 'There! Another one!' I was very upset for the man who had brought back the book because it wasn't fair, and I said 'That's the same tear!', and I was frightened when I heard what I said because I didn't know whether I'd said it outside or inside, and I had to have a good novel for Mammy.

Everyone buys hens from Mrs Garber. If you don't know her, you say 'the hen woman'. They are white or pink or yellow, with bright yellow claws, because she sits on the curbstone and pulls their feathers off. And sometimes they have little golden balls inside that are eggs. Mammy cooks them with the chicken soup, and I love to eat them. But I don't understand how they are eggs, because eggs are white as well as yellow, and they have shells on.

Prune stones look like little black beetles, and where bits of prune are still sticking to them, it looks like little legs. I don't like to see them.

The tops of tomatoes look like spiders. I'm not frightened of spiders, but when Ellie puts a tomato top down my back and pretends it's a spider, even though I know it's a tomato top he *makes* me frightened because he expects me to be frightened, and sometimes I feel I should be, and I am. Even though I'm not.

I keep reading about *The Little Match Girl*, and about *The Red Shoes*. How cruel it has to be, being a little girl.
　But I need to know.

I come home from school and go straight into Sidney's house. He is always in the front room, playing the piano. There is a big armchair in the corner, and I climb right into it. I am very quiet. Nobody looks for me for a long time.

We went to the Maypole shop, and they had Cinderella's coach all made out of butter. I always wonder what they will have, when I go. How do they make it? It is on the marble counter, that is always very very cold when you touch it. We have a marble table at home, that the jug of water and the basin stand on, and that is always very cold too. And swirly. Marble is swirly.
　I hate it when you have a cloth dipped in the cold water in the jug and rubbed on your face, and they hold you so that you can't move. Grown-ups are always holding you so that you can't move. Other times, when you might want it, they don't touch you.
　The coach is pale gold. I've seen flowers that colour, I don't know where. I think when we went to Mrs Butterworth's and the bellowing cows.

Mrs Gramovski is sitting on her step, talking across the road to Mrs Taylor. Mrs Taylor sits on a chair in her doorway. Louis puts her there every morning before he goes to work. She is blind, but she hears everything. She always knows what you are doing, and who it is doing it. She is like God.

Bobbie Goller has two barrels of pickled herrings, and two barrels of pickled cucumbers in her sitting-room. And bottles of wine and med on the shelf. People buy them. You have to have money to live.

I like med very much. You have a bit in a glass and then someone squirts in soda water or lemonade if you are little. It tastes like *satisfaction*. I don't care if you can't say that. I know that's what it tastes like. *Satisfaction*. Like the end of a sentence.

We have a big ball like a moon outside our house, because Daddy is a doctor. It says Surgery. When I was little, he was a teacher. I don't remember that, but Edna says so. She says she didn't live with us then. He learned to be a doctor in the evening, because he had been a soldier in the war, and he was allowed to, Edna says. Actually it must have been the night, because in the day he was being a teacher at Derby Street, and in the evenings he had his cheder, and a lot of the time as well he was in shool. People come and sit in the hall, and say they're on the panel. If they're uncomfortable, they could just move their chair. Aren't they allowed to?

I hate having to go to the cheder. Sometimes Mammy sends me with a message. All the boys turn round and stare at me, and flick ink pellets at me, and laugh, and bounce up and down on the benches, and shout things, and Daddy keeps hitting them across the head, and says angrily to me, 'What do you want?' He always hates seeing me.

When you want to stuff pillows or peronies you buy a sack of feathers from Mrs Garber, and put them in the oven by the side of the fire. Mammy won't tell me why. Edna says it's to kill the fleas. I don't understand about fleas. What are fleas?
    One day I was helping Mammy make the bed, and she

suddenly took hold of the edge of the sheet as if she was hiding something, and pinched it tight. So I said 'What's that?' But she wouldn't tell me. And when she took her thumb away, there was a little black smudge on the sheet, and I said 'What is it?' because she was frightening me, and she didn't want to say what it was but at last she said it was a flea. Is a flea a smudge, then? I can't understand how it can't have any thickness, but only be a smudge.

I listen to Sidney playing the piano and I don't have to say anything, just listen, and Sidney just plays.

Mr and Mrs Cohen came and had tea, and I saw a smudge on the white tablecloth. I thought it was a flea, and I was afraid Mr and Mrs Cohen had seen it, because you mustn't see them.

I don't really understand how fleas are smudges and not thick. Can people be smudges?

Wickets are the lines boys chalk on the wall when they play cricket. There is a good wall round the corner in Hilton Street. Bails is the bar they chalk on top.

I think that is what ghosts are. People smudges.

Mammy has made me a book-list to take to the library, for myself. I give it to the big lady, and she goes into the little back room, and finds me one of the books on it, and crosses it off the list. *Eric, or Little by Little*; *St Winifred's*, or *The World of School*; *Four Heads to Furnish*, or *The Crown of Success* and ever so many more. There is always 'or'.

I keep seeing flea-smudges everywhere.

Monty is one of the big boys. He's bigger than Ellie. He lives down Peru Street. He's got a puppy, a brown puppy, and he let me stroke it, and its fur strokes the wrong way. You have to stroke it from its tail up to its head. I don't know why it is. It's the way it goes. It worries me. Nobody will tell me anything.

It's all right to have a dog. Once Bobby Cohen had a dog, but now she has chickens. But not greyhounds. Greyhounds are Christian.

Three boys got hold of me in the school playground, and said 'You drink baby's blood, don't you.'

Outside a horse fell down, and the man whipped him to make him get up and he couldn't. He tried and tried, and sparks came out of his hooves. I can't bear it when someone falls down and can't get up.

When people keep saying you do things, you begin to think you do. Perhaps in your sleep. People can kill people in their sleep. Without knowing. Or like Mr Hyde, in the story that Ellie and Sidney talk about. Because they keep on saying that you do them, even though you say you don't.

Today Mammy asked me to tidy the top of the dresser, and somebody had spilt some tea-leaves. I was just going to pick them up in my fingers and put them in the teapot when Mammy grabbed my hand tight and made me jump. She shouted in a horrible voice 'No! Don't touch them!' Then she said 'They're mice.'
    How can they be mice? How can tea-leaves be mice? Like smudges are fleas! Nobody ever tells you anything. They just shout as if it's something terrible that you've done.

The grit chases round on the flagstones like Monty's puppy chasing its tail. It leaves a swirling pattern on the ground.
    When you crouch down to play ogdens or marbles, the dust leaps up suddenly and bites your eyes.

Girls aren't supposed to play ogdens or marbles. Only boys are.
Girls are shouted at because they should be inside skimming the
chicken soup, or pulling sheets.

Whenever I see tea-leaves now, I don't know if they are mice.
How do other people know?

Today Sidney was playing on his piano and he put his finger on
the bottom end, and zipped it right up to the top, like on railings. It made my back shiver. I said 'Do it again!' and he laughed
and he did it. But the first time he did it, it was in the music. I
looked at it, but I couldn't see where it was.

I am sitting on Sidney's wall, and I can see the scissor-grinder
with his wheel that sparks and spits and sizzles. And I can see the
ragman's donkey, but not his cart, because only his head is in the
entry.
      He has a sad face, the donkey. All donkeys are sad, even when
nothing is happening. They remember sad things. And the ice-
cream cart is coming, with its fluttering canopy. Can-o-py . . .

I hate it having to count the coalman's sacks, and be his enemy.
Standing at the window, watching.

Ogdens are cigarette cards. We say cigarette cards, not ogdens.
They have pictures on the front and they tell you things on the
back. I have a set of butterflies, and half a set of cricketers, and
some wild animals. I like things that tell you.

Sidney has a wonderful game. You have a lot of pieces of cardboard and they have questions on, and wherever a question is
there's a hole, and you put the piece of paper over the box, and
the box has little metal stumps that stick through the holes in the
paper, and you have a sort of wire like a long bootlace with a tag
on the end, and if you touch the tag to the right answer it goes
BUZZ. The pieces of cardboard have questions and answers

about all sorts of things, and there are so many of them. It makes me very excited. Sidney and Ellie play it all the time, but sometimes Sidney lets me play with it. It's an electric game, like boys have. Girls aren't supposed to.

Killing Jesus

1924

Yesterday two boys got hold of me in the playground and banged my head against the wall over and over, and said 'Why did you kill Jesus?' I don't know who they thought I was. My head hurts.

I keep thinking about stroking the puppy the wrong way. Actually it's the same way you get the scales off herrings. You take hold of the herring's tail, and you take a knife, and you push the scales up to the herring's head, and they fly off like sparklers. You have to hold tight because it's slippery. The scales are brilliant silver, and they fit together as though a very clever dressmaker had fixed them for a bridesmaid's frock.

The scales fly everywhere when you do it – on your clothes, into your hair, over the pots and pans, everywhere. And the herring's head is bright red – scarlet – and it looks very beautiful with the bright silver and scarlet. But I know the scarlet is blood really, and it's because it's dead. Ellie is playing with Sidney. Boys don't have to do herrings.

★

Wallflowers, wallflowers, growing up so high,
All you pretty flowers will soon have to die.

You sing that in a line, facing the wall. Then you turn round and sing:

'Excepting somebody, the sweetest of them all,'

I don't mean you *say* 'somebody', you say someone's name, and then you turn round, and flick your frock up to show your knickers and push out your bottom and wiggle it as if you were hitting someone with it, and then you sing:

I'm ashamed, you're ashamed,
Turn your face to the wall again.

It is a very sad song.

There are two kinds of birds, big ones that are pigeons, and little ones that are sparrows.

The sparrows eat the straw in the street. Sometimes the straw is horses' mess that has been flattened out by the cartwheels, and dried up. The sparrows like it.

I saw one find a bit of bread that someone had dropped. I was very quiet, and its crunching was as loud as shouting. The pigeons are like rainbow puddles.

Big girls often flick their frock up to show their knickers and push their bottom at boys and make an ugly face at them over their shoulder and wiggle their fingers. Then the boys throw stones at them.

Round the corner of Sidney's house, in Hilton Street, where the other sweetshop is that doesn't have Devon Cream toffee and the things grown-ups like but lots of things for a ha'penny, there's a family with ever so many children in it. I don't know their names because they're Irish and they're Christians. There isn't anybody Christian in our street; except the Davidsons. And last night their dad was fighting all the grown-ups in their street. They were all shouting, and some of their faces were bleeding. And their mammy was walking along singing very loudly, and her friend was walking with her, holding her up because she kept falling over, even though the friend was much littler than she was. And her little girl was walking behind, and she was screaming because she was frightened, because her mammy had changed. I can tell her mammy wasn't generally singing and laughing and jolly. And the little girl was very frightened because she had suddenly changed and was jolly.

Clogs are Christian.

A telegram is when someone is dead.

In Great Clowes Street I saw a telegram boy on a bicycle with a message, and I stood quite still. Everything went very far away.

In Lewis's I have seen a lady fold up a piece of paper and put it in a little box. And she puts it on a wire and shoots it along to another lady. And the other lady takes the box off the wire, and takes out the paper and opens it and reads it.

I have looked and looked at the telegraph wires in the streets. If I am shopping with Mammy, I always watch them as we walk along. When I am by myself, I go to the bottom of Fenney Street and put my head right back till my neck hurts, and I watch the wires. But I can never catch the boxes rushing along the wires with their messages saying someone is dead.

Do they only go at night-time?

But what about Lewis's?

★

Do they say someone is dead in Lewis's?

Jam and custard is like the sunset. I draw in it with my spoon, making bars of orange and swirls of purple, and the blackberry pips make deep blue speckles in the gold. The sunset is like jam and custard.

It is my favourite, even better than tinned peaches or pineapple. We have it for breakfast on Shabbos morning, because you don't have to cook it, and because it's so lovely.

Christians hit everybody. Other men. And women. And children.

Jewish people hit only children.

Ellie knows lots of things because he's older than me. But he won't tell me. And when I say 'Tell me! Tell me!' he laughs and says he doesn't know. But I know he does. He just won't tell me.

Mammy gives me some white net, to sew beads round. There are lots of beads, and I can put any colour I like. Then they go over the milk-jug or the sugar-basin. When I see them on the table, I feel I am belonging.

If I made them for everywhere, then we wouldn't have to have the flypapers. The flies buzz and buzz, until they die.

But I would have to make so many, all different sizes, hundreds of them, millions of beads. I don't think I could do that.

Today Sidney let me take his electric game to play with on the sofa. I was playing by myself, and Daddy came downstairs, and I looked at him because I couldn't help it, and he looked back, his black look, at me. He hates me.

When he'd gone, Edna was in the room and she said, 'He isn't angry with you, pet. It's because your Mammy's just had a baby, and it's been born dead. It's upset him. It was another boy, and he wanted another boy.' I didn't know she was having a baby. Is he very angry with Mammy for killing the baby? I'm sure she didn't mean to.

Edna tells me things, sometimes.

I'm making some mats to stand things on. Like the teapot, or Mammy's scent bottle on the dressing-table. It doesn't have scent in, but it has a lovely smell. I do blanket-stitch all round, and in the middle I do yellow daisies. I like choosing the colours better than doing it.

In Albert Park, if you look down the hill at all the trees, there are so many colours, but all green. How do people know they are all green when they are all different?

The blood doesn't show very much. It's only specks anyway.

I say 'anyway'. I think you don't say 'any road' if you want a good education.

Sometimes − not often, but at special times − he gets out the magic lantern, moving the slide slowly. He does it for Ellie. He doesn't look at me.

I don't really like reading letters to people. I can read them, but sometimes I don't know what it means, and I don't know if I'm saying it right. Mrs Sugarman sits in her rocking-chair, and nods her head, and says 'Read that again, chuck', and I do read it again, but it still doesn't sound right, and I don't know what it is. But Mammy sends me to do it because it's a blessing.

They come from America, the letters. That's farther than London. In London it's Piccadilly, but here it's Piccalilly.

It isn't Haroloid. I thought it was like celluloid. But it's Harold Lloyd. That's his name.

There is a box made of shells, that is magic.

And there is a box like a dark-red mirror, and inside the lid a little square where it says First Prize for Needlework.

They are Mammy's boxes.

We have an ice-cream bucket, to make ice-cream out of Bird's Custard Powder. It's yellow, and thick, and it makes a sandwich with the wafer biscuits. Daddy does it. He does any special thing.

The Stop Me and Buy One Man is at the corner. He sells very special ice-cream for the grown-ups. Sometimes grown-ups give you the ice-cream paper to lick, and if you don't they say you're sulking. I don't like it. It makes me feel sick.

I'm going to get a Snofrute from him with my penny. I squash it on the cardboard and lick it off. It stays on your tongue like a tuning fork.

Mrs Garber sits on the edge of the pavement and plucks hens. There are feathers everywhere, drifting with the grit and blowing in the wind and heaping up in soft silky swirly piles – white feathers, brown ones, orange, black. Even red ones.

Today I saw a brown wispy one on her nose. It was curly like the curly horn of Roland in the picture when he raised it to his lips and blew. It *tickled* her, so she flicked it with her hand. Flick! Like that! But there were feathers all over her hand, so now there were *more* feathers on her nose, red and white and brown feathers, curling, and fluffing out, and dripping, as if her nose was running feathers!

Then she sneezed. And they flew away.

> *Felix kept on walking, kept on walking still,*
> *With his hands behind him,*
> *You will always find him,*
> *Blow him up with dynamite but him you couldn't kill,*
> *Right up in the air he flew,*
> *He just murmured Toodle-oo,*

Landed down in Timbuctoo,
And he kept on walking still.

They always play that when there's a *Felix the Cat* picture.

I can't bear the way they wet the corner of their handkerchief on their tongue, and rub it on your face because you've got a smut. It *smells*. It's really horrible. I try to get away but they always hold you tight.

Edna is going to get married, and not be here any more.

They are building the bonfire in the yard. Everyone is dragging bits of wood down the entry and putting it on the pile.

The chair where I sit when Sidney plays is in a soft dark corner. The music is like a summer afternoon, with bare feet on the hot flagstones, and water near with a chained cup.
    Sidney played it again today, He said it's Spanish. He told me who wrote it. The name is like water in summer too.

Christians beat boys and girls. Jewish people only beat boys. That is because they think only boys are important. But Christians think girls are important enough to beat too.

Today Miss Reilly said, 'All the Jews stand up on the forms.'

We had fireworks in the yard. Not *our* yard. I mean the big yard, that's for everyone.
    There were lots of sparklers that we could hold in our hands; and they fizzed with cold stars. And rockets shooting like corks out of bottles of med, and exploding in the sky. And Catherine wheels spinning with colours. And then something terrible happened. A banger chased me. Somebody let it off and I knew at once it would come after me and it ran at my heels, snapping and barking, and I ran as fast as I could and I ran into our own

yard and I ran into our lavatory. I was afraid it would come through the gap under the door, but then I would climb on the seat, and if it jumped on the seat I would have to jump into the lavatory, and if it came after me then I would die.

But it didn't see where I had gone. I waited a long time. When I came out, all the fireworks were over.

They lit the bonfire. I like the crackling, and the flames leaping, curling and twisting in the dark.

Then I saw they had put someone on top of the flames, and they were shouting and laughing. I wanted to scream but I don't know how. Edna looked at me and said 'It's only a guy. It's made of rags.' But it turned in the breath of the fire and it held out its hand to me, *begging*. Edna said 'It's made of rags. It's only fun. It's because they burned a man years ago.' But to *do* it! To remember, and to *do it again*! And to *laugh*!

I don't like On the Floor and a Bit Higher. You tie one end of the rope to the lamp-post and somebody holds the other end. At first the rope lies on the pavement, and everyone can jump over easily. But it gets higher and higher. Until you fall. That's the only way it can end, when you fall. There isn't any other way.

I play it because everyone plays it. You have to.

Because I Am Seven

1924–1925

Two big boys got hold of me in the playground and pushed me against the wall, and said 'Say "ch"'*. So I said 'ch', like he did. Then the bigger one said 'There!' and he banged my head against the wall, and he said 'That shows you're Jewish.' Then the other one banged my head too, and they both ran off.

Mammy says I'm not going to Grecian Street School any more. She says I'm going to Derby Street, because that's the Jews' School.

Derby Street's the other way. Not through the park. Not through the autumn leaves.

It's along Bury New Road, past all the cloth shops. Then you walk up a long hill, past factories that smell of raincoats.

No more leaves, crimson and gold, with their patterns like

* as in 'loch'

crushed hopscotch chalk, and the way they stuck to my shoes that were wet with the shuffling through.

We don't have Edna any more. We have Phoebe.

Monty Filver has something magic. It is a brown box. He brought it out on the step and sat next to it.

He had something on his head like a hairband, with things over his ears. I thought it might be something big boys wear in shool.

I stood very close to him. And suddenly he took the thing off his head and put it on mine. There was a lot of sizzles and sparks of sound like frying chips, and then I heard a man say in my ear that his name was Jack.

I play whist. And snakes and ladders, and ludo, of course, and put-and-take with used matchsticks, but grown-ups don't play those. Only whist.

Ellie and Sidney have a box like Monty's. It is called a crystal set. They stroke something called a crystal with a cat's whisker. Is that really true, a cat's whisker? People either won't tell you anything, or they tell you lies.

Did the cat mind or did they just take it anyway?

Mammy says it won't be long till I'm seven, so I don't have to go into the Infants. I can go straight into the Girls. I'm glad because Miss Myers is the Infants' teacher at Derby Street and she's been to our house, and she has too many teeth and she laughs like a wolf.

> *Home in Pasadena,*
> *Home where grass is greener,*
> *Where honey-bees*
> *Sing melodies*
> *And orange-trees*

Scent the breeze.
I want to be a home-sweet-homer,
There I'll settle down . . .

'Where grass is greener' makes me think of the leaves, the leaves on my shoes.

When Bobbie Goller makes taiglech, it's just like a proper table-cloth that hangs down, only it's dough.

Once I was under the table in our house with a real proper tablecloth that hangs down, and Phoebe screamed. Everything went far away. She ran out of the room and her scream stayed, and it was like a faraway train at night. And once I was under the table, and Mammy said I was secretive. How could I be being secretive when I was just happy under the table?

She cuts off all the hanging-down part with her knife, and puts it on the slop-stone. Then she makes tiny little square cushions, and she puts them in jars of golden syrup, and they'll stay there for years and years. If you eat one, it is hard outside, but the golden syrup leaps suddenly out, and it is a surprise every time even though I know and I am longing for it.

Once Mammy had visitors and there was a box of chocolates and the visitor said I should take one, and it was hard outside and soft inside, and the inside flooded your mouth like taiglech and it was a surprise though I almost guessed it.

Grown-ups don't like you being quiet, or by yourself, or thinking.

Phoebe stays in her room in the evenings, and talks out loud in a horrible hissing whisper that you can hear everywhere in the house, even though her door is shut. Mammy says she is praying. I can't tell any words. But every one is like a hissing stab, a cruel and killing stab. I think she is trying to kill everyone with her praying. But she does it in her room, like sending out a spell. When she hisses like that, I can't move, not even my hand.

★

I think Phoebe is afraid of living with us because we are Jewish. She makes me afraid too. I think when one person is afraid, everyone is, even the one they are afraid of.

I saw an aeroplane *write* in the sky. How did it do it?
It twisted and twirled to make letters, but no one fell out.
And when it had made the words, it flew away, but the words stayed there in the sky, and I watched them till they began to fade away . . . Daily Mail . . . aily Mail . . . ily Mail . . . ly Mail . . . and my neck hurt. It was so beautiful.

Miss Rose Wolf is my teacher. She hits everybody. With everything she can find. Blackboard stick, ruler, book, anything. I don't know *why* she hits them.

She doesn't like the way they talk. They're really used to talking Yiddish. They don't talk English very well. I think it drives her mad the way they talk, because she wants everyone to be better educated, so she hits them.

Today she got hold of Yetta Silverman's arm and held on to her *tight* and she turned back her sleeve from her wrist and made her hand go into a fist, and she got hold of a ruler, and began to beat, beat, beat on her knuckles, over and over again. Yetta was screaming and trying to pull her hand away, but Miss Rose wouldn't let her and kept on beating her and Yetta kept on screaming, and Miss Rose was beating and screaming too, mocking her.

Today I found something very strange left on my bed. It was stiff like iron, and bent round as if it was starting to be a hoop, and it was dark-red and smelled bad. Phoebe came and snatched it away from me, and said 'It's mine.' I said 'What is it?' She wouldn't tell me. So I said it again and at last she said 'You wear it on your body. Women do.' I said '*Where* on your body?' I couldn't see how it could go on your body, because of the way it was stiff and bent round. And she wouldn't tell me, again she wouldn't tell me, but at last she put it round her waist – not her waist – round her chest – without saying anything. I still don't understand because I can't see how it fits or how it fastens.

Anyway, I'm never going to put on something that smells like that, when I grow up. They can't make me. I'll go on wearing liberty bodices as long as I live.

Christians always say that Jews are so clever because they eat fish. But can't they eat fish too? Or aren't they allowed to?

I'm going to make a flicker-book of my own. You draw Charlie Chaplin standing on both legs on the first page, then standing with one leg a bit off the floor on the next page, then with it a bit more off the floor . . . And when you've done all the pages you flick it very fast and Charlie Chaplin DANCES!

I can't do it. I can't draw.

I keep thinking of that aeroplane writing in the sky. Like a train puffing out smoke.

Trains are sad. Because of the whistle. When I am in bed but not asleep I hear the trains whistling. It comes straight to you through the night like an arrow. The train is lonely and I want to cry.

On the way to Derby Street there is a very long, very high wall. It is the wall of Strangeways. Strangeways is the prison. It is a wall to stop the people in there from ever getting out. Inside the wall they sing the Strangeways Prison song. 'If I had the wings of an angel, out of these prison walls I would fly.' But they can't.

Sidney let me put on the hairband thing. It caught in my hair, but I knew I mustn't speak. I must stay absolutely still. He stroked a lot with the Cat's Whisker, and kept turning a knob, and then there was crackling and hissing and I knew something was going to appear out of fire and smoke. And suddenly a voice said 'You, Hello. You, Hello.' And I said 'Hello' back very softly.

Is a crystal to do with a Christian? But we're Jewish. Perhaps we shouldn't have it.

Mammies and daddies and aunties and uncles talk Yiddish, and they also talk English.
  'Make nice,' all the grandmothers say. When a little boy is pulling a cat's tail, they get hold of his hand and straighten out the fingers and pull it over the cat's fur, stroking it, and they say 'Make nice. Make nice.' They do it when a little boy pulls a girl's hair too – 'Make nice.' I think it should be 'Make nicely.' Or something.

I don't speak Yiddish.

I hear grown-ups talking Yiddish, but I don't listen. Like the horse didn't listen this morning when Mr Barr was talking to Mrs Glodowski. He just flicked his ear. He knew he wasn't talking to him. When people speak Yiddish, it means they're not talking to me. I'm not there.

Daddy beats Ellie with the tawse. But he gives him presents, all sorts of things, that we can't afford. Mammy says so. They are always quarrelling about it. He beats him because he's so important to him.

Today Mammy said 'When you're seven, you can learn to play an instrument. You can choose between the violin or the piano.' I said 'Which is harder?' She said 'The violin.' I said 'I'll choose that.' I knew I had to make her happy.

A lot of things have to happen when you are seven.

Because I am seven, I have had to be sent to hospital to have my tonsils out. The hospital is a big bare room full of children with nothing on and all crying because their mothers had left them there, and all sitting on enamel chamber-pots all over the floor, and the nurses shouting at them and slapping them because they haven't done anything in the pots. 'You'll do something all right!' they shout. And the children scream.

When I woke up the children were all in cots, still crying but sadder, and the nurses were still screaming. My throat was like grated horseradish. I cry without any sound.

A Motion is Number Two. That's what they say in hospital – 'Have you had a Motion?'

A lot of people have Scottsy Motion.

The most horrible thing about Opening Medicines is the way they pretend to be Licorice Allsorts. I don't mean you think they *are* Licorice Allsorts. But they pretend. But you know they aren't.

At home, I have Cod-liver Oil and Malt, Parrish's Food, and Syrup of Squills. Really it's Syrup of Almonds, Syrup of Violets, and Syrup of Squills, but no one has time to say it all. I love it, the smell, and the taste, and the colour. It is *so* purple. I have never seen anything so purple, except that Mammy has a purple cape with white swansdown round the edge that she wears for people's weddings and sometimes for shool. And Parrish's Food is very beautiful too, like a jewel. And it tastes like metal. Actually I've never tasted metal, so I don't know how I know that it tastes like metal.

Actually, sometimes I've licked the bed-knob.

And Cod-liver Oil and Malt is a beautiful shiny brown, and you can turn it over in your mouth with your tongue. You can say Malt Extract if you like. We don't have Virol. I don't know why. I think it's something to do with wanting a good education, but I'm not absolutely sure. Or perhaps Virol's Christian.

It can't be Christian, because Eta has it.

It's Scott's *Emotion*. Not Scottsy Motion.

I don't think it's fair that boys can do it anywhere they want – in the gutter, down the grid, against the wall, on the lamp-post, anywhere at all, just whenever they feel like it – and girls aren't allowed to. They have to wait till they get home, even if they wet their knickers and get smacked. Boys can do it higher and higher on the wall just for fun, and they try and beat each other, and sometimes they even go right *over* the wall and they laugh and dance about and are very happy when it falls on someone on the other side who shouts at them.

When the sun shines through it, it's like a rainbow – all colours. And the drops fly out like bright fireworks.

I've tried at home, standing up and pulling at it, but it won't go the same. It just falls downwards and makes your socks wet.

> *What's your name?*
> *Mary Jane.*
> *Where d' you live?*
> *Down the grid.*
> *What number?*
> *Cucumber.*

I saw the label at the chemist. Scott's *Emulsion*.

Daddy talks to Ellie but he never talks to me. Mammy talks to me, but she talks to Ellie as well, though not so much as Daddy does.

Daddy talks *about* Ellie – in front of him, I mean – but Mammy never talks about me. Except once Mrs Galansky said

'What do you use to get your floor so shiny?' and Mammy laughed and said, really proudly, 'Leilie's elbow-grease.' What's elbow-grease? I've never heard of that. Anyway, she knows I do it with floor-polish, of course.

I've never heard her say anything proud about me before.

Moving Staircase

1925

In school, we're reading a book called *The Old Curiosity Shop*. Everybody has a turn at reading aloud. You can't turn the page. You have to wait for each person to read. They can't read very well, and she screams at the person and hits them.

I try to look down at the page, like a horse with blinkers on, and just see the words, but I can't. I still see what is happening.

Yetta and Zelda and Evvie and Angie eat locusts all playtime. They get them through the railings from the toffee-man, with a tray round his neck. Zaidie Goller used to be a toffee-man outside the railings, but I was very little then. He sold the sweets Bobbie Goller made to the children through the railings. Was I even born?

I read in a book that locusts are a sort of grasshopper. Well, if they are, of course I don't mean *that*. People don't chew grasshoppers, do they?

I have two Licorice Allsorts in my pocket. One is the kind that's covered with hundreds and thousands. I don't like that kind really, because it looks like Opening Medicine. But the other is a kind I love. It is all black, with a thick white overcoat of snow. They get covered in fluff, because of the pockets. Mammy makes the pockets and sews them in the side of my frock. And I don't know why, but there's always fluff in the corners.

I can't keep them anywhere else. I can't keep them in my knickers because these knickers don't have a pocket. And you can't put them in the leg-part where the elastic is, because Licorice Allsorts move around.

Uncle Izak came. He took the kettle off the fire and put it straight on the white tablecloth. He always does that. Mammy started to say 'Don't', and Uncle Izak and Daddy shouted at her, before she'd said it.

Uncle Izak is in the *Jewish Chronicle* again this week. It is always writing about him. It calls him the Stormy Petrel. Petrel . . . not Petrol . . .

Mammy and Daddy were quarrelling about Uncle Izak and the kettle in their bedroom last night. I always try not to hear, but their voices fly all over the house. It's like Phoebe's hissing. That was very soft, but it still flew all over the house. I make the voices go very far away.

Miss Rose doesn't hit Queenie and me. She calls us the scholar-ship ones. It's much more frightening when everyone else is hit and you're not.

Her sister, Miss Kate, is worse. I think they're both mad.

She always puts a big red tick on my compositions, and writes 'Excellent'. I write what I want. It's like going for a long walk away from the hitting and the screaming.

★

Last Sunday we went to Liverpool to see Uncle Izak's new house. All over the floor is a huge map of Palestine. I mean the floor is a map. It's called mosaic. Mo-sa-ic. Uncle Izak has put tiny little pieces of stone together, ever so many different colours, to make a map. It covers the whole floor, so you can't help walking over it but any minute Uncle Izak might shout.

And there are little statues everywhere that Uncle Izak has made from wood. They are not like ordinary statues. They are wild, like tigers are wilder than cats.

And in another room there's a printing press for making Uncle Izak's books and pictures. A printing press. That's what it's called, a printing press. You can call it just a press, and you can say he works the press, but he's not a presser like Uncle Joe who spits on the iron.

The pictures are made with black ink, and they are very jabby like his beard and shouting like his voice. Even the little ones.

Ellie and Sidney buy notebooks at Davidson's and turn them into magazines. They write stories and poems in them and do funny drawings and crosswords and questions. Then they lend them to each other. They have names. They won't let me see them, but I do sometimes.

All last week there was a very thick fog. It lasted eight days. When you wanted to wipe your nose, a hand came by itself out of the fog, wiped your nose, and disappeared into the fog again. It was like *Grimm's Fairytales*. We had to write a composition about it. I started 'It began on Monday and finished on a Tuesday.' I just said 'it'. I never said 'the fog' all the way through.

When I hold the skein looped over my two thumbs, with my fingers stuck out, and Mammy winds it, I sway from side to side like a dance, twisting and turning, without music.

★

When we pull the sheets it's the same. There's no music, but the drums are playing, and cymbals.

I don't mean *really*. Not *really* playing. But when you pull the sheet, *hard* and suddenly, twisting your body, it makes a thudding, cracking noise, like gypsy music.

Sometimes, especially if it's Ellie, the other person pulls very hard, and pulls it right out of your hand on purpose, and laughs, and spoils it. I hate that.

Sometimes Mammy gives me the wool for me to hang round the top of a chair, and wind by myself. Then I wind it without dancing. Just winding.

When people are dipping, some people say:

> *Eena meena mina mo,*
> *Sit the baby on the po,*
> *When it's done,*
> *Wipe its bum,*
> *Eena meena mina mo.*

But people like Queenie and me say:

> *Eena meena mina mo,*
> *Catch a nigger by his toe.*
> *If he hollers let him go,*
> *Eena meena mina mo.*

I think it's something to do with reading books and being well-educated. I think teachers like you better if you do the second one because it's more educated. But how do they *know?* They never hear us say it.

I don't want to see the story of *Hansel and Gretel*. I never have wanted to see it, ever since I've been little. I don't understand how people can write such cruel stories and have them made into books, so that they can be in libraries and be left lying about anywhere for anyone to see.

How can a father take his two children into a dangerous wood, and leave them there? On purpose? For ever? How can they make that into a book, and just leave it lying around for anyone to see, suddenly?

I was in Bury New Road and Mrs Abrahamson stopped me and said 'How's your Auntie Sadie, love?', and I said 'She's very ill. She's in hospital.' And Mrs Abrahamson laughed and said 'She's not ill, love. She's having a baby.' How does Mrs Abrahamson know she's having a baby?

I've got a big book, called *Our Darlings Annual*. It's from a secondhand shop. I think it must be a magazine, *Our Darlings*.

There's a story in it about a little girl whose mammy is always making her work very hard. And another little girl moves next door, and she asks the first girl to come to play. And she hears the new girl ask her mother something, and the mother just smiles and says 'Just whatever you like, my dear.' And the first girl goes home again, and after a little while she tells her mammy how it was in the other house. And then later on her mammy is going to tell her to do something, or to be some way, when she stops and instead she says 'Just whatever you like, my dear,' and smiles at her. The first time I read it, I cried. To myself, I mean. Now I've read it over and over, sitting in a corner by myself, and I keep crying. I cry right from the beginning now, because I know what's going to happen. I can't help it.

I don't mean out loud. Nobody can hear me. Tears just go on trickling quietly down.

A lot of people have carbolic soap. We have White Windsor. I think it's something to do with having a good education.

I don't like carbolic. I don't like that red colour. And I don't like the smell either. I don't like smells that say very loudly 'We are going to make you clean.'

But I don't like White Windsor specially either. It always has sharp rusty bits in it that you can cut yourself on.

When I'm grown up I'm not going to have chopped-up soap. And I'm not going to have an old rusty knife to cut soap up with. I'm going to have soap in beautiful smooth rounded shapes, each shape on its own, each one a different colour. I've seen soap like that in Kendall's windows when I go to Town with Mammy.

Why do children in books always say mummy, when real children say mammy?

Last week I got my foot caught in Bobbie Cohen's grid, the big one, in front of the cellar window. I couldn't get it out. It was a long time before someone saw me. In the end, the fire engine came, and a fireman with a helmet cut through the bar.

When something happens and you can't do anything you're supposed to shout for help. I don't know how to do that. And how can I when you're supposed not to make a fuss, and to wait quietly?

I was in Cheetham Hill and I saw two dogs stuck together. It was terrible. They were back to back, and somehow they'd got stuck together and couldn't get separate, and nobody was caring about it, they were just laughing, as if it didn't matter at all to get suddenly stuck together. And then someone went and got a bucket of water and poured it all over them and they came apart. I was so thankful, because I was very frightened. It might happen to anyone. But people still laughed.

Uncle Joe talks Yiddish but he talks Russian too. That's because he was in the Red Army. I heard someone say 'Fancy, a Jew allowed in the Red Army.' I hate 'allowed'. Uncle Joe is Daddy's cousin, not really my uncle.

Uncle Joe presses trousers in their front room, and the room billows with steam. Billowing is not the same as bellowing. He spits on the iron – a big fat spit – and it bounces off like hard little marbles.

His iron is so heavy I can't possibly lift it. I tried. It holds on to the table like with a magnet.

Ellie and Sidney have magnets. Girls don't have them, but Sidney showed me how if I rub Mammy's fountain pen on my sleeve lots of times, it will pick up bits of paper. It's as good as having a magnet, he says. Sometimes I tear up a little pile, and the pen picks up a huddle of them, all clinging together, like the feathers that day on Mrs Garber's nose, or the geese in the story about the Goosegirl.

I heard Daddy tell Uncle Percy that when Uncle Joe came to England he tried to get him to learn English just so he could read where the tramcar was going. But he wouldn't. He just smiled and said 'God will look after me.' Daddy said Uncle Joe was always saying 'God will look after me', and what he meant was he – that's Daddy – would look after him. When he was telling Uncle Percy, he looked angry but pleased at the same time.

Listen! An aeroplane! I'm going out to see.

I like the moving staircase in Lewis's. But what would happen if you didn't get off at the top? Would you go underneath and get flattened out like sheets in the mangle? When I get on, I start getting ready to get off, in case I miss it.

Phoebe said she was going to be sick, and Mammy was *horrible* to her. She said 'Don't you dare be sick in here!' as if she was hitting her. And Phoebe was frightened and said 'No, no, I won't, Mrs Goller.' And Mammy pushed her out of the kitchen as if she was a cat or a dog going to be sick on the floor.

Today Phoebe said again she was going to be sick, and Mammy

pushed her out, *horribly.* People can't help being sick.

I am learning motor-cars. So far I know Bentleys, Rolls Royce, Daimlers, Baby Austins, Morris Cowley, Morris Oxford, Fords, Wolseley, Armstrong Sidneys. *Sidleys. Sidd-e-leys.* They are all on cigarette cards.

If you wet your finger and rub on the part of an old cigarette packet where it used to be fastened together, an aeroplane will come. I mean, a *drawing* of an aeroplane. You have to rub very gently.

Then you have to send it away, and you get a hundred pounds.

I don't know where you send it to.

How do people know about these things? How do you learn how to know? Everyone is picking empty cigarette packets up, from the pavement, and the tops of tramcars.

Because it's Purim Daddy is taking the cheder to the pictures. It's a Purim treat. I can go too. I am the only girl.

We have it all to ourselves. When we go in, we get an orange. Orange-peel and paper darts are flying through the air and Daddy is shouting and hitting boys' heads all the time. But at last it starts. *The Ten Commandments.* The air smells of oranges.

Mr and Mrs Cohen and Mr and Mrs Galansky come to play whist in our house, and they have sandwiches on plates with doyleys. That's paper cut into patterns. It's nothing to do with Gilbert and Sullivan. The silver ones are best because you can wipe them over with a damp cloth and use them next time. If they have grease marks on, like the white ones, you can't.

Auntie Sadie and Uncle Percy have moved to Leeds. I'm staying with them for the holidays. I'm going in the coach by myself. Mammy says she'll ask the conductor to see I'm all right.

★

Auntie Sadie has drawers full of tiny little tubes, tiny little bottles, tiny little boxes. As if they're for tiny little people.

Or perhaps they were once ordinary size, and someone changed them to tiny because of something they'd done.

This morning I had a look at some that were in the dresser drawer, because Auntie Sadie asked me to get her a fork. And they were Tomato Ketchup, Reckitts Blue, Amami, Californian Poppy, Raspberry Jam, and Vanishing Cream. Is that what made them tiny?

I know how Auntie Sadie gets the tiny things. Every single evening she sits at the kitchen table, and writes her name and address on different parts of the newspaper, and posts it. Then the tiny things come. They are that size to start with.

Auntie Sadie has cream soda, and lime-juice-and-soda, and dandelion-and-burdock, and sarsaparilla, as well as Vimto. We only have raspberry and orange and things like that. I wish we had Leeds pop.

Auntie Sadie is always sending away for things. I am going to send away for a fountain pen with Ardath cigarette coupons. Uncle Percy used to smoke Ardath cigarettes, and he is going to give me all the coupons he has saved for years and years.

It is my last day at Auntie Sadie's, and my fountain pen came! It is so beautiful. It is not black, like Mammy's Swan fountain pen. It is jade-green and gold. Jade-green is not like any other green. It is green with milk poured in it so that it is very gentle and calm, and it has two gold bands and a gold nib. It is the most beautiful thing I have ever seen. I will keep it for ever and ever, and I will remember that Uncle Percy gave me all his coupons for it.

The Girl Who Doesn't Know How to Scream

1925

The nit lady came today. Yetta was standing next to me. Becky Salomon was in front of her. Yetta said to Becky 'There's a huge insect climbing up the back of your neck, into your hair. It's got eight legs and nasty green horns. It's really horrible. Can't you feel it?' Becky screamed and cried, and Yetta laughed.

I've started my violin lessons with Mr Cohen. They've moved to Broughton Park, now. Mr Cohen has a toilet roll in his new house. I could see Mrs Cohen was very excited when she showed me where the lavatory was when I hadn't asked for it yet.

I knew what it was as soon as I saw it. You tear it off along the little holes. Only there's nothing to read on it.

I expect you could still take your book in, though.

The thing is, they only have boys, no girls, so there's no one to tear up the newspaper. I expect Mrs Cohen always had to do it herself in the old house. I tear ours into squares – I try to tear them the same size, but they generally come out different – and then I make the holes, and I thread a piece of string through the whole lot, before I hang them on the hook. Some people don't bother about the string. They just have a hole, or not even a hole. But I like the way it looks. And orange papers are so soft and smell so beautiful. Sometimes I make a pile of them, and I hold them to my face before I wipe my bottom.

Every so often, Mammy gives me a bucket of hot water, so I can scrub our lavatory seat. I like the way the seat goes dark when you wet it, and white when it dries, and the way the soap-suds go swirly. I write my name in the suds, but I have to wipe it off again.

I don't think the Cohens' lavatory is wooden. It's black and white.

Actually, where would you put the book? There isn't any side to the seat.

On the floor, I suppose.

Sidney writes things down for me. Tunes, I mean – things I like – Spanish music that is full of sun – so that I can play them on the violin. He writes very fast, and his notes are very delicate neat little pin-headed people. Mine are clumsy-looking and ugly and I write very slowly and have to think all the time.

I wonder if anyone has written down Salford drizzle in notes, or riding on top of a tramcar when it's pouring cats and dogs, and there's no one there but me. Loving it.

Ellie has won a scholarship to the Manchester Grammar School. Daddy is very pleased. He talks about him a lot. He is going to spend a lot of money on him.

★

Yetta said to Becky Salomon today, 'I can tell you've got a false bottom.' And Becky cried. Can people really have false bottoms? How would they manage when they went to the lavatory?

Mr Cohen gave me some sweets after my violin lesson. He'd wrapped them in tissue paper. I said 'Thank you very much.' But when I looked, I saw it was lavatory-paper. I could see from the edges where it was torn along the holes. It made me feel sick. I couldn't eat them.

Outside the church in Montagu Street there's a man nailed to a cross. We're not supposed to see it because we're Jewish but I can't not see anything. It says outside the church that God *gave* his very own son to be nailed on the cross because he loved him. And it says he *gave* him to the world to nail on the cross because he loved the world. How could God do such dreadful things?

I think there are men nailed on crosses outside all the churches. I can't understand how Christians can bear to look at them. It shouldn't be allowed, to show such cruel things.

Every time I brush my teeth, I see the Gibbs Dentifrice castles. They grow like a cluster of flowers, but in the clouds.
Cluster . . . that's like snuggling up to each other.

There are prayers for everything . . . eating bread, drinking wine, seeing a rainbow, waking up in the morning, wiping your bottom, washing your hands. No, not prayers. I mean thank yous. Thank you God, for giving me back my soul in the morning. Thank you God, for remembering about the rainbow and your promise. Thank you God, for helping all this stuff to come out of my bottom.

I hate how the old men with long white beards blow their noses with one finger against it, right on to the pavement, or on to the floor of tramcars. The same with gobbles of spit.

It's better on the tops of trams. They don't come up the stairs. And I like sitting there in the rain.

Gobbles is a nice word. Or is it gobbets?

The seats on the tramcars have wooden slats and the backs can face whichever way you want. When the trams go back the other way, you just push the backs over. The back of the seat only covers the back of your shoulders. Underneath, where your bottom is, there's a space. I always sit on top, because I like sitting in the wind and the rain. But often men sit behind me and stroke my bottom through the space, and I wish they wouldn't. I don't know how to stop them.

I read the story of *The Boy Who Didn't Know How to Shiver*, in *Grimm's Fairytales*. I am The Girl Who Doesn't Know How to Scream. I think anyone could jump out at me with a knife and I wouldn't be able to call for help. I don't know how to do it.

It's all right for Jewish girls to have new straw hats with ribbons for Pesach, if they're *short* ribbons. If they're long ones, they're Christian, like Whit Walks.

Whenever I see anyone push back someone's sleeve from their wrist, it's like a flash, and I go cold.

Miss Faust said 'Put up your hand if you need a new coat for Pesach.' Yetta and Zelda put their hands up. Yetta got a blue one with a cape, and Zelda got a green one with a sort of astrakhan bit round the neck. Mr Michaels sent them from his factory.

Yesterday Mr Seckler sent shoes for the boys. Yetta said so. Sometimes what Yetta says is true. Sometimes it isn't.

Yetta Silverman and Zelda Shimansky were rushing down the road, and Yetta was shouting 'My mother will *murder* me if I'm late!'

★

'My mother will *murder* me if I'm late.' I keep practising it in my head. I don't mean practising so that I remember it. I mean to see how it sounds. If *I* say it.

I said it out loud today. I dared to. Just once. But I won't ever again. All the girls looked at me, and I felt very ashamed because they knew I was pretending, and just wanting to be the same as them.

When I'm grown-up I won't have best clothes and ordinary clothes. And I won't have milk plates and meat plates. Or Pesachdich plates and plates for other times. And I won't do the washing always on Mondays.

Friday Night is Amami Night.

It is nearly Pesach. I am standing on a chair, helping reach down the Pesach wine-glasses. I take one in my hand and I jump off the chair. And the chair and me fall together on to the floor, and the glass smashes into my hand, because I am holding it. It is bleeding terribly.

Mammy is getting Daddy. I hear his feet coming. He tells me to get up. The tap is too high for me. It doesn't matter when you wash your hands ordinarily, but holding it up like that for a long time hurts. He holds it under the cold tap for a long time. He won't let me pull it away. When he lets go, I feel a cold ache. Nothing else.

He takes a penny out of his pocket, and he gets a bandage, and he bandages the penny and he puts it against the middle of my hand where it's bleeding. And he makes me clench my fist on it very tight. It is like a hard stone. Then he bandages round and round my fist till it is a huge snowball. It is bigger than my face. How can I hold up such a huge hand?

I can see he likes it. He ties a scarf round my neck and puts the snowball in it. He likes that too. It is very tidy-looking and dazzling white and beautiful.

★

Pesach is about leading the children of Israel out of Egypt, out of slavery. You can call it Passover.

Everyone will come to our street for the nut games. It is an important street. There are more holes in our street than in any other street. They come for a whole week. Like going away for your holidays.

Everyone is kneeling or lying or crouching on our pavement. Is that right, crouching? Or is it couching? The grown-ups have to walk in the road. And I am looking through the window. Really it's the boys who play. The girls mostly keep the bowls heaped high with nuts on the sitting room table, so that the boys can come in and get some more. But soon I am going out. Because only my left hand is bandaged.

Cupky's really for little children. You have to put three nuts together near the wall, with their points touching, and you put another on top. Then people come along and roll a nut to try to knock the cupky over. If you do knock it over, you get all the four nuts for yourself. It's really for babies, or girls who have to keep clean.

The one you play in the holes, I think it's really for people who don't want a good education. You have to whisper Yiddish things to your nuts. 'Bubbele . . . Boychik . . .', you have to say. And you have to rattle them round in your hands, with your mouth bunched up, like kissing. And if they don't win, if they don't stay in the hole but come bouncing out like children, and run wild and laughing all over the pavement, you shout at them 'Shtik naar!' Daddy shouts that sometimes at me, if he ever does speak to me. It means 'You fool!'

Then you rock them in your hands as if you're praying, And then you spit on them. And the last thing is you do a big kiss up into the air, and say 'Boychik', and shake your head with your eyes closed, as if they are so wonderful it hurts to talk about them.

★

You have to have a shoe-box for the important game. I mean the one that people play if they're supposed to get a scholarship.

Sidney's mother has shoe-boxes because she's a dressmaker. She keeps spangles in them, and tassles, and cottons, and buckles, and buttons, and if she's not there you can run your fingers through the spangles and they're cool and slipping, like water. Generally she is screaming at Sidney and chasing him with a hairbrush, but at Pesachtime she's nicer for a bit. She even gave him a shoe-box. She has even given Ellie one too.

You get a pair of scissors and you make four holes in the corners of the lid where it stands up high, and you write the biggest numbers over those, like 4 or 5, because hardly anyone can get a nut into them. And then you make other holes all over the lid, and you put only little numbers over those because everyone will get nuts in there. The one in the middle is the easiest of all, because the cardboard goes down like a skipping rope between the lamp-posts, so you write 1 over that. Then you put your box against the street wall, and wait.

I can see it makes people feel quite different, having their own shoe-box. I would like to have one, instead of just watching, and keeping the bowl full.

Uncle Percy took me to see the Whit Walks. He took me and he lifted me up and sat me on a lorry so that I could see everything, over the heads of the crowd, and yet be safe. There were flowers everywhere, and the children in white, walking along the tramlines and over the cobbles, holding the long long ribbons that are fastened to high-up faraway banners with names like Eccles, and Ancoats, and Hope, and Pendleton, and Irlams o' th' Heights, all rippling like the field of corn near Mrs Butterworth's, and sometimes clapping and banging like when we shake the blower to make thunder for a play, or when we stretch the sheets. And the streamers, look! Skittering and frisking in the wet gritty Salford wind! Skit-ter-ing . . . The girls in their long white dresses, and the flowers in their heaps and in their garlands and their baskets and their bunches, held to their body like babies, and their beautifulness all out in the open, with everyone watching all out in the open. And the girls are queens!

Uncle Percy doesn't mind the children are Christian, and the banners are Christian, and all the grown-ups watching and being happy are Christian, even though he has a cheder of his own like all my other uncles, and knows about all the rabbis, and speaks Hebrew, and when he talks they all listen. All my uncles have cheders and are ministers or chazans. Auntie Sadie wants to call him Peter, but he says no, why should he change his name. His name is Percy.

Today Daddy unwound some of the bandaging so that he could put some more on, so that it would go on looking snow-white and beautiful. He says that way my hand won't have to be stitched, so it won't leave a scar. He is very pleased with the snowball. I can see he is proud of it.

The M.D. Class

1925

School holidays. Bare feet on the flags. They almost burn you.

Mary told me that where she comes from there is no work for anyone to do, and no one has any money. Specially miners haven't. You have to work to have money. And you have to have money to live.

Sometimes there's a Disaster, and people are buried in the mine, and their mothers and their wives wait, with scarves round their heads, crying. I see the pictures in the *Manchester Guardian*. They make me go cold inside, but I still have to look at them, because I have to know.

All the grown-ups are sitting out in the street, on the doorsteps. Sometimes on a chair on the top step. Mrs Kaminsky does that – sits in a chair. Auntie Sadie says she thinks she owns the street. Just because she has a fur coat.

Mary comes from Glasgow. Edna came from Wales. That's quite close. Sometimes when it was her day off, she took me home with her. Phoebe came from Rotherham, I think. Those are all places where there's no work, and people come to live with us and do the fires on Saturday. Mammy always sees they go to church and the Girls' Friendly Society. I think that's something like the Temperance Billiards Rooms. It's a Christian place to go.

All the girls are bouncing balls, and cocking their legs over. You have to practise that.

> *One two three alara,*
> *I saw my Auntie Clara*
> *Sitting on a pomdelara*
> *Eating chocolate soldiers.*

Pomdelara . . . is that right? I think it's one of those big fat round things, with a belt round the middle, and you sit on it instead of a chair. People with pianos in the room often have them. You have to say it at the same time you cock your leg over.

I have an Auntie Clara. I mean really. She is married to Uncle Hymie, and their children are Minnie and Lilian, who send the clothes. They are rich. That's why they live in London. All the people in London are rich. Mammy says Uncle Hymie ran away to sea when he was fifteen and got to South Africa on a ship and looked for gold. He is her favourite brother, because he is so kind, she says.

> *Oh the moon shines bright on Charlie Chaplin,*
> *His boots are cracking*
> *For want of blacking . . .*

You can bounce a ball to that too. But against the wall, not on the flagstones. How do people *know* what to do?

What's Dardenelles?

★

Mary says she would take me home with her, to have tea with her family, but it's too far to Glasgow on her day off.

Boys always jump up on the backs of carts, and ride there, till the man sees them and chases them off. Girls aren't supposed to do that. It can't be because it tears your knickers when you slide off, because doesn't it tear boys' trousers?

Daddy unwound the top bit of bandage, and put some clean on.

You have to have someone if you are Jewish because you can't poke the fire on Shabbos. But I don't understand this because in the Bible it says you and your man-servant and your maid-servant and anyone that is in your house must rest on the Sabbath, not just you. I've said this but no one will listen. I don't understand why they make you read it and learn it if they don't want you to know.

Today our class went to the Art Gallery. But we mustn't look at Christian pictures.

Can Jewish birds sit on Christian churches?

I don't understand why people tell you to always remember something and then tell you it isn't like that. Or show you things and then pretend they aren't there. And other people say you've done things when you weren't even born. I don't understand why we're taken to the art gallery when most of the paintings we can't look at. It makes me angry. And it frightens me.

Yesterday Miss Nathan sent me with a message to another class. She often sends me. I don't think the other girls like her choosing me. Well, I don't like being chosen.
I have to go through different partitions, and sometimes I can't find the door through – all the bits look the same. And when I go through, everyone in the next class stares at me.

And I have to hurry, but also I have to go slowly on tiptoe – till I get to the partition on the other side of the room, and go through that one.

But this time, it was playtime, and there weren't any classes on the other side of the partition. Except, there was a class in Miss Lucy Cohen's room. That's the M.D. class. M.D. is short for Mentally Deficient, but you say M.D.

Miss Lucy was reading to them, about someone called Eeyore, and Winnie the Pooh. I began to walk very slowly because I wanted to listen, and I began to walk even quieter than I generally do because I didn't want her to notice I was listening. I have never heard those stories. I have never heard of a teacher reading stories to children in such a soft gentle voice, and being with children when it isn't a lesson-time. But in the end I had to go through the next partition. I couldn't stay any longer.

At night, I prayed very hard to God, 'Please God, make me Mentally Deficient.'

My bandage has been on for three weeks. Today Daddy unwound all the bandage. Then he said 'Open your fingers!' And I couldn't. He took hold of each one and made it open. I cried. I couldn't help it. I didn't make any noise. He opened each one flat, and then he got Ellie's ping-pong bat, and he bandaged my hand against it. I have to have it like that for a long time. He likes the way it looks. He says that way it will heal without leaving a scar.

> *Oh the Blues, the jolly jolly Blues,*
> *The Blues shall live for ever,*
> *The Reds shall die,*
> *With a carrot in their eye,*
> *And the Blues shall live for ever.*

Brian Paisley sings that, and sticks his tongue out at me, and pulls my hair. Mary says I should say back:

Sticks and stones
May break my bones,
But words can never hurt me.

Reds means Liberals. We're Liberals because we get the *Manchester Guardian*, and we go to the Liberal Shool (that's synagogue) and we vote Liberal and we go to the Liberal Summer Schools in the country. All my aunties and uncles go. I love the buttercups and daisies, and climbing the stiles. Styes are not the same as stiles. And shool is not the same as school, but a bit like.

I said to Uncle Percy what Mary told me, and he said 'Words *do* hurt you'.

I am the person who has to write to Enid Blyton. Enid Blyton has a magazine called *Sunny Stories*, and she writes to children in schools and says 'Please write back to me'. And Miss Rose has chosen me to do the writing back.

'Natives' means black people. Natives don't wear clothes, and they have spears, and they are dangerous and they don't have any education.

A new girl has come to school. She has very fair hair – not a reddish colour like me but yellow. Not browny yellow but greeny yellow. Cut in a bob with a straight fringe in front. Like Julie, but his is dark. I think perhaps she's Christian. But she can't be, if she comes to this school. Maybe her mother is Jewish but not her father. Her name is Yiven. Like 'given', but with a y.

Today Daddy took off all the bandage. I can't bend my fingers or move them from side to side, but he got his black look and said I will soon. There is a scar across the middle of my hand. He says it will fade. It *must*, because it makes him hate me.

I don't think *she* says Yiven. I think she says something else. But everybody else says Yiven. You write it Y-V-O-N-N-E. She is very pretty. I like looking at her.

Daddy is building the succa in our yard. He has planks of wood and a saw.

He is tying bunches of grapes and apples and oranges to the ceiling of the succa, and flowers, and so many leaves of different greens. And they hang down, and the sun flickers through them like confetti in front of churches. I see it when I go on the lavatory. I walk around the succa and in at the lavatory door. He doesn't speak to me and I don't look at him.

You can't see the succa on the lavatory. Even if you leave the door open, you can't see it, because the door gets in the way. If you could look at the succa while you are sitting on the lavatory, then you would know it was really a special time, like you are supposed to know and remember it is a special time, instead of ordinary times when you read a square of newspaper or a book, and don't look out of the lavatory door at all. But the door gets in the way.

Succas is the Festival of Booths. Booths . . . what's that? It is so that we remember when the Children of Israel wandered about trying to find a home, and built tents to live in, in the wilderness.

You can call it Tabernacles . . . What's that?

Daddy has put the table and the chairs into the succa. We are going to have our tea in there. Everything. Breakfast, dinner, tea. And on a little table, that is really the whist table for when Mr and Mrs Galansky and Mr and Mrs Cohen come, he has put the bunch of willow, and the myrtle, and the palm leaves, and the golden lemon- no, not a lemon, but something like a lemon, on a cushion of cotton waste like an old lady's hair. That is so it stays absolutely perfect. Because it has to be perfect.

Mrs Taylor has an empty scent bottle she lets me smell sometimes, a very tiny one. Just for a moment. Then she puts the stopper on again. But there is no stopper on the succa. I open my nose, and smell it all the time I am having tea, and I eat the smell too, the smell of the willow, and the myrtle, and the palm tree, and the golden lemon that sits on its white cushion, that is called . . . what is it? . . . A *citron*. Perhaps it is called a citron, not a lemon, because it sits? Instead of hanging from the tree.

I polish the apples till the red shines as if there is a glowing light inside. Then I wash the glass bowl with washing-soda water, and it flashes like diamonds. I've never seen diamonds. But once when we were rambling in Matlock the wind blew and the stream went into crinkles like when Mammy is setting jam, and every crinkle flashed in the sun. That is 'like diamonds'.

I put the apples in the bowl, carefully, so that every apple is in its right place. The red right, the green right, the yellow right. It doesn't matter that I can't polish the oranges or the bananas, because sometimes colours are right and even lovelier without a shine, like hopscotch chalk. Then I put it in the middle of the table, with the white cloth spread all round it.

This afternoon, Mr and Mrs Galansky and Mr and Mrs Cohen are coming. Mammy says I must pass things round.

Changing from Minor to Major

1925

Mammy sent me to Boots to ask for a packet of towels. I said 'What sort of towels?' You need to know what sort. She said 'Just say "a packet of towels".' She said 'The man will know.' I don't understand what sort of towels they are. They are fastened up in a little packet. She won't tell me.

I always have a sore throat and I can't swallow. It feels as if something is stuck there.

We're in St Anne's! We came on a train! St Anne's! With the clock made of flowers, and the pen that writes a jagged line for the weather and you look at it every morning, and there's miles and miles of sand, loose sand, that piles up in high slithery hills with grass sticking out like needles out of knitting, and you stagger about and you fall in it and it doesn't hurt, and there are rabbits popping in and out of it, and flowers, so many flowers, and the wind blows through your hair, and your eyelashes are covered with sand, and right at the end of the sandhills, of the lane called Happy Valley . . . *Happy Valley* . . . there's the pierrot show! It's always there. Every day . . . And you all sit down on the flattened-out sand holding your balloon or your windmill, and you sing the St Anne's song.

> *St Anne's! St Anne's!*
> *Where the couples do the courting*
> *And they soon put up the banns,*
> *By gosh! It's posh!*
> *And the air's as rare as*
> *any time at Cannes.*
> *Go there and never die,*
> *You feel just like a lad of ninety-three,*
> > *and*
> > > *though*
> > > > *the*
> *Girls may not be wild,*
> *They're the smartest in the Fylde,*
> *At St Anne's-By-The-Sea.*

And then the show starts.

On the pier, where you sit and listen to the music, there are glass tables, and underneath the glass are doyleys . . .

What's banns? Perhaps it's *bands* . . . Soon put up the bands?

I love the Floral Hall where the ladies' orchestra plays, and the flowers grow down from the ceiling like stalagmites, and the flowers grow up from the floor like stalactites, and they hold out their arms to each other. Or is it the other way round?

I saw caves once, where there were stalagmites and stalactites, and it was so cold, and water was trickling down somewhere. For ever after . . . That's how it felt, the water trickling thinly down the rock . . . for ever after . . .

> *By gosh! It's posh!*

And the air's as rare as
Any time at Cannes.
Go there and never die.
You feel just like a lad of ninety-three . . .

That doesn't make sense. Feel just like a lad . . . ?

The seashore pebbles making patterns all the way to the sea. And the roses. I pick up the petals and hold them against my cheek, and they are *cool*.

Feel just like a lad of ninety-three . . .

The Gardens at St Anne's are a bit like Albert Park. The rockeries, the lakes, and the bridges like eyebrows, and the men playing bowls, kneeling.

If an old man lay in the sand-dunes, his beard would wave in the wind like the starr grass.

You feel just like a lad, *at* ninety-three! Yes!

I've been away at The Fresh Air Home for a week, because of my throat and my nose. It's at Delamere. I didn't like it there. It was terribly cold and windy. I didn't know anyone. All the girls could Charleston except me. You have to be very loose to Charleston, and I've got stuck tightly together somehow. And one of them sang 'I want to be happy' without any music, and did it straight off, without thinking even. I wish I could sing it like that. But when I look at the music and the way the bar-lines come, and count in my head, and work it out, it's hard. It was exciting the way she sang it. It's called syncopation.

I can sing through all *Iolanthe* in my head – the accompaniment bits as well – and all the *Mikado*, and the *Gondoliers*, and the

Pirates of Penzance. Sidney copies out bits for me to play on my violin, in his tiny thin little pin-men.

I like *Odon Olam*. That means Lord of the World. It's an evening song. Sometimes I sing it in my head before I go to sleep, before I send my eyes up in my head or rub between my legs. 'Into his hand I commend my spirit, both when I sleep and when I wake. The Lord is with me, I shall not fear.' That's what it means in English. I sing it in Hebrew in shool, but we have English on one side and Hebrew on the other.

The tune is like sitting alone on top of an open-deck tramcar under a grey raining sky, and suddenly a ray of sunlight shines out of the sky like a torch. I sang the tune to Sidney, and he said it was changing from the minor to the major. I don't know what that is yet.

I like using the brush-and-crumb-tray, when visitors have gone. The brush part is very soft and silky like a friendly animal, and the tray has little daisies painted on it, red, white and green.

I stroke the brush on my hand because it's like having a pet, and then I shake it on the white cloth, and sometimes the crumbs jump in the air, just for fun, and I have to be patient with them.

Mr Cohen keeps giving me sweets in toilet paper after my lesson, but I never eat them. He doesn't know I don't eat them.

He has two boys. I think he would quite have liked a girl.

I sang *How Lovely Are Thy Dwellings Fair* to Sidney. That's one we sing in English. He said it was a tune that had already been written and it hadn't anything to do with *How Lovely Are Thy Dwellings Fair*. He said it was by . . . someone, and I just can't remember who. I asked him again today, and he can't remember what he said. I keep saying 'Tell me, tell me!' but he says he can't remember. He *must* remember!

★

The medicine I have now – the taste, the smell, the colour, make you sick almost. And it makes bumps under your skin that hurt. It's called Bromide and Valerian. I heard Daddy say my nerve ends are too close together.

In our schoolbook and on the blackboard it says 'The cow gives milk.' 'The cow gives meat.' That's horrible. The cow *doesn't give* it! It's cruel to say that. Why do grown-ups say such cruel lies? And then they make children learn them!

My throat is always sore so that I can't swallow. It is like a huge lump that gets in the way – a rock. But when I open my mouth for someone to look, they say they can't see anything. But there's *something* there!

On Yomtov – that means a festival – some women smell horrible. I don't know about the men, because they're downstairs. I don't know what it is that's smelling. I thought maybe it was their fur coats, because some people have fur coats, and I think they only get them out for Yomtov, and the rest of the time they're covered up in a wardrobe, so maybe it's mothballs. But we have mothballs – not for fur coats – Mammy doesn't have a fur coat – but for blankets – and they don't smell like that. They rattle around like marbles in the bottom of the cupboard, and sometimes shoot out like mice when you open the door.

Mary says she knows someone who works in a hairdresser's and you can have something done to your hair at special times to make it wavy, and *that* smells horrible. Is that what it is? Is that what they've done? I'm glad I'm not God, to have people stink for my sake, and pretend I like it.

The Picture Spoke!

1926–1928

Today we had to fill in sentences. 'The wind howled over the roofs like . . .' I put 'like the cry of a soul in agony.' Mine all got a tick, and 'Excellent!'

I said to Sidney again today, '*What* did you say that tune really was – *How Lovely Are Thy Dwellings Fair?*' And he said 'I don't remember. I don't know.' I said 'You *do* know. You told me!' He laughed, and he shook his head. Why do people who know things not tell you? Even Sidney does it.

Sermons are sometimes boring. But I think of something of my own, or make up a poem. Anyway, quite often they're something interesting to think about. Actually being in shool is as good as reading on the lavatory for a long time without anyone rattling the knob and getting angry.

I don't understand about Jacob. He was a horrible man. But at the same time he was wonderful, and we should always praise him. How can they say that? When they've just read about how horrible he is and told you to read it?

Auntie Essie and Uncle Simie and Phil have come to stay, from London. They talk quite differently from us. Phil is one year younger than me. He got his socks dirty, and I got told off for it, not him. They said I was responsible for him because I was a girl. I just don't understand that. And I scarcely even know him! He's horrible, anyway. And he talks very whiny. Daddy said 'Bay windows!' He said it when they weren't near. All the people in London talk like that.

London is where the pavements are gold. Gog and Magog live there, in the British Museum. Can they still be alive, then? Prisoners in the British Museum? Is that possible? I saw about them in the *Children's Encyclopedia*, but I didn't have time to read it properly.

I know now why the children in books always say mummy, not mammy. I've thought about it for ages, and now I know. It's because they say words differently in London from the way we do. When they mean to say 'Come', it comes out 'Cam'. So when they say 'mammy', they really mean 'mummy'. No, that's not right. It's hard to work out. It's like a sort of secret code. I keep thinking about it, still, – why they write mummy in books – because I haven't got it worked out quite right. But that's why it is – the way they talk. It must be that. There must be a reason.

I hate the way grown-ups pinch your cheek! It *hurts*. They laugh when they do it. And if you don't laugh, you're supposed to be sulky and you get told off. Sometimes it makes my eyes water.

There was a student driving the tram today. He kept banging the bell with his hand and laughing. I thought it must be the Students' Rag, when all the students dress up in funny clothes and come up into the trams with the RagRag and collect money, but Mammy said no. I said, 'Then why is a student driving the tram instead of a real tram-driver?', but she wouldn't tell me. Why won't people tell you things? They know, but they won't tell.

Hatikvah is the Song of Hope. The music is so sad to start with. Then suddenly it jumps up and marches away down the road with a banner! It's what Sidney said – changing from the minor to the major.

I keep having this dream, of me in a sledge, rushing over the snow. It's very cold, with ice everywhere. And wolves are howling and trying to get close. I keep throwing meat out of the sledge to try to keep them satisfied so that they don't tear me to pieces. But I'm always afraid I won't do it in time.
  Or am I awake when I have it?

I can't do a tremolo. Mr Cohen keeps getting hold of my wrist and shaking it in the air to try to make my hand flap about. He says if it came loose I would get a tremolo, but it stays stiff and clenched up. He doesn't shake it hard. I think he's afraid he might hurt me.

In the *Manchester Guardian* and the *Jewish Chronicle*, judges . . . or is it magistrates? . . . anyway they're always saying that if all parents treated their children like Jewish parents do, and really cared about them getting a good education, their children would never get into trouble and be sent to prison.

I still keep having this dream. About the wolves. You have to have something else to throw out. Because the very last thing is me myself.

Raymond Cohen is a year younger than me. He can do a tremolo. His hands are square, and his fingers are short and stubby, and their tops are flat with no nails sticking out. That's not the way they're supposed to be if you play something, short and stubby.

Boys play football in the street. But if you're a girl you have to stay in and help make the beds and pick up their clothes that they've thrown on the floor, and skim the chicken soup. And they have barmitzvahs and get piles of presents – silver hairbrushes and Brownie cameras and leather wallets and Blackbird fountain pens – and grown-ups queue up to shake their hand – just for being thirteen. Girls are thirteen too!

And they draw on the walls 'Follow this line', and you follow it, and at the end it says 'Evvie loves Abie' or 'F—— the Reds.' What's F——?'

The Cohens all say 'fiddle', not violin. Everyone who *plays* the violin, not just listens to it, says 'fiddle'.

Or do you have to be Jewish *and* play the violin to say 'fiddle'?

Ellie and Sidney get the *Magnet*, and the *Gem*, and the *Popular*. They get them between them and they swap them. Sometimes they get *Sexton Blake*, and sometimes *Wizard* as well. They leave them about, and I read them. I know bits off by heart.

Yetta and Ray and Milly are always talking to each other about things that are happening in girls' papers. There's a Bessie Bunter in one of them – she's Billy Bunter's sister. I think maybe lots of them have sisters in the girls' papers, but I don't know, because I would never read them.

Cecil and Raymond Cohen have a gramophone. I've never asked if I can wind it up, because I don't think they'd let me. They have gramophone records of Misha Ellman and Yehudi Menuhin and Galli Curci and Albert Sammons and Jelly d'Aranyi and Gracie Fields and George Formby. Cecil is afraid Gracie Fields will hurt her voice because she hasn't had lessons like Galli Curci. I know someone called Galli but he's a man. He has sleepy sickness and another illness too. He's one of Daddy's friends. I think they went to Manchester University together. Not actually *went to*. They were allowed to learn to be doctors when they weren't doing anything else, because they'd been in the war. It's called extra Muriel. Galli has supper with us, and he can't manage his knife and fork because of sleepy sickness, so we all eat without knives and forks to make him feel better. I don't think this can possibly make him feel better to see us all making a mess and dirtying the tablecloth and feeling frightened about it. But we have to.

A long time ago, when Uncle Galli was well, and I was little, he brought us a rabbit. Daddy had a party for himself and he invited all his friends who had been in the army with him and gone to Manchester University. He made cards that said it was a Surprise Party, and everyone had to bring a surprise. Uncle Galli brought a big pie, and when Daddy cut it it was cardboard and a white baby rabbit jumped out, and everyone shouted. Ellie and I kept it. We had it in a hutch in the backyard, but one morning I brought it a lettuce leaf, and it wasn't there any more. There was a hole where the latch was, and chewed-up splinters all over the floor. I had never thought that it didn't want to be with us. Perhaps it was a Christian rabbit.

On Sundays, everyone in Salford and Manchester gets on a train and goes to a buttercups-and-daisies place, and you ramble. Ramble . . . that means wander about.

Inside the Maypole, where you get butter, there's a big picture on the wall of a little boy and a little girl. And the little boy is holding a buttercup under the little girl's chin, and saying 'Does 'oo love butter?' That's the way it's written down – 'Does 'oo . . .' And you can see the gold shining on the underside of her chin, and that proves she does. It tells you. Like pulling petals off daisies and saying 'he loves me, he loves me not,' and it tells you. I've tried to do this to myself to find out if I love butter, but it's hard to see in the mirror when your head's tipped back, so I don't know.

In Town there is a shop called The Invisible Mender.
But I *saw* her. She was sitting in the middle of the window, stitching something. She was absolutely clear!

I was frightened to say anything to Mammy about the invisible lady. Mammy was talking to me when I saw her, but she didn't know I was frightened. I don't say anything to anyone when I see things that nobody else seems to.
There were a lot of people standing in front of The Invisible Mender's shop. They were all staring, trying to find her. I could see her quite easily, through the tram window. I keep thinking about it.

I like going to Matlock and Buxton and Crich and Middlewood, but not so much when Miss Myers comes too. She smiles at me too much. But most times she goes to Windermere with her painting easel. Sometimes we go there too. Sometimes we have a Summer School – that's what it's called, Summer School, but not like Sunday School which is for Christians – and they are all grown-ups except Ellie and me.

My cousin Philip Smith is going to be at the Summer School this year. He's a grown-up. He's Mammy's cousin really. His mother is Aunt Smith. That means she's Mammy's auntie.
Cousin Philip is a Liberal candidate. That means you ask people to choose him. Someone called Stafford Chips is going to be there too, a very important person. Cousin Philip Smith doesn't say anything, and he doesn't do anything. I mean he doesn't, on purpose. If you are a candidate, that is how you are. He has a brother, cousin Harry Smith, who is a dentist. And he has another one, who is the one Aunt Smith likes best. She calls him 'My Sidney'.

★

This afternoon she said in the street that My Sidney had made a lot of money selling a lorramanoor. I don't know what that is. It is a beautiful word. Perhaps it is a parrot. With a tail curling over like those party things that Mr Davidson has in his shop window. You have to blow them very hard, and they open up straight, and then they curl up again. Or perhaps it's a wild man of the mountains who leaves huge footprints in the snow.

Even the grown-ups didn't know what it was. Mr Slotki asked out loud, 'What *is* a lorramanoor?' He sounded as if he was frightened of it. And she said 'A lorramanoor? A lorramook!'

I still don't know what it is. And what is a lorramook?

Sometimes people pretend to tell you, but they don't tell you anything. They just say anything so as not to tell you.

It's Stafford *Cripps*. I'm glad I didn't say it out loud.

I found out today that all this time it's been *sord*. I mean it's written sword, but you say *sord*. I feel terrible about this. I don't think I ever said it out loud, just said it in my head. All the time it was *sord*, and nobody ever told me.

This year we went to *Ben Hur*. I mean Daddy took the cheder there, and I went too.

It was terrible the way he beat and beat the slave. They went on and on beating him but he was already dead and his heart had burst. I can't stop seeing him.

Miss Nathan invited me to tea at her house. Her niece, Estelle Wein, was there, and we all had tea together. Estelle Wein was very beautifully dressed, and had tea with her finger sticking out. I think she must be rich. She is having piano lessons with Solomon, in London I think. She says Solomon says she should play only with her fingers, not with her arms. She showed me what he meant on Miss Nathan's piano. It's very quiet and gentle, stroking the keys like a little pussycat. Like 'Make nice'.

I didn't say anything at school about having tea with Miss Nathan's niece, but somehow the other girls know, and they say I'm schteiff. That's stuck-up. Just because she's the headmistress.

Yesterday I took someone into our house. I invited her. Children do it in books. Mammy was very angry. She was changing the plates over to the Pesach ones. She shouted, and I pulled the other girl out into the street.

Everyone in our street went to Town to see *The Jazz Singer*. (Not Mrs Taylor. But Louis went.) It spoke! The picture spoke! Everyone was calling to each other in the seats. I was afraid they wouldn't stop calling when it started. This is the first time ever in the whole world a picture has spoken.

The grown-ups were crying all the time. All the way through. Especially when he sang *Mammy*, and *Kol Nidre*. They were crying and wiping their eyes. Everyone thought when he sang *Mammy* he was singing to them, that they were his mammy, and he was their boy. When they came out, they were saying 'A Yiddishe boy, nu!' as if they were very happy. But they were still crying.

Just one grown-up crying makes you cold inside, because you need them to be happy. But they were crying at the Mammy song and being happy at the same time. I don't understand it.

It's funny. Really, I have a lot of relations, but they're far away. I mean, they live near, but they seem to be far away, even when they're in the same room.

Yesterday Solly Bernstein was sitting on the flagstones outside his house, and he found some ants. He said he was going to capture them and give them to Belle Vue. He got a lemon-tea glass from his house, because his mammy wasn't in, and he put it over them. But he couldn't think how to lift them up. I was kneeling on the pavement too, looking at them, and thinking how to lift them up, and they began to be like my aunties and uncles rushing about, and me looking at them through the lemon-tea glass.

That dream. I keep having it. In the end there'll be nothing left but your own self.

I've just read two books, one after the other, and they're both about a girl in a boy's school. In one, she's called Taffy. In the other she's called Tazy - that's short for Taisez-vous. You say Tazy-voo. It means 'Shut-up' in French because that's what the boys are always saying to her. At the moment I like all names that start with T. Taffy and Tazy, of course, and Topsy, and Tilly, and Tammy. I choose those names for my children when I'm thinking I have them.

They're always the headmaster's daughter. That's why they're the only girl there. They're just as brave and daring as the boys, and they do just the same things that the boys do, and when they get caught and they're caned they keep their chin up and hold their head high the same as the boys but more haughtily. And even if a tear squeezes out of the corner of their eye they don't make a sound.

I go through all the stories when I'm in bed. I make up my own too. And I rub my special place and I go to sleep.

Sometimes when I'm twisting my special place, and being caned the same as the boys and holding my head up high, the master takes hold of my chin and tries to make me look in his eyes but I pull my chin away. And then it clicks over the top and I fall asleep.

Sometimes I have the public flogging the same as the boys. Sometimes I don't manage to fall asleep wiggling my special place, so I have to do the looking-up-behind-my-eyes way, until my eyes click over.

I wonder why schoolboy always means someone rich. I don't mean only in stories. In the *Manchester Guardian* it does too. So what are people who go to Derby Street or Grecian Street called?

★

Today is the day for the scholarship results. The big scholarship, not the ordinary ones. I thought the postman would bring a letter about it, and I thought my mother thought so too, but she didn't say anything. I didn't say anything either. Anyway he hasn't come and I have to go to school. At prayers, Miss Nathan says 'We have very good news this morning. We are very proud of Queenie who has had a letter this morning to say she has won a scholarship to the Manchester High School.' Everyone claps. The clapping sounds far away, and very slow, like the roundabout stopping in the empty fairground.

I don't know what happened after that. But after a while I saw my mother was talking to Miss Nathan. I don't know how she got there. I didn't see. She must have come in through the door. And then I hear Miss Nathan saying 'And here is some more good news. The postman has only just now come to Leila's house, and she also has won a scholarship to the Manchester High School.'

My mother goes away. I think people must have clapped again.

Miss Rose is near me, and she says 'You have made your mother very happy.' The horses inside me start to move again very slowly. Up and down, up and down.

Tangerine Slices

1928–1929

We've moved. We've got a new house.

I like this house. It's a house like I always draw, with the door in the middle, and two windows on top and two windows underneath, and all the curtains looped back, and a chimney with smoke scribbling out, and a garden with roses in it, and a fence all round. Only I can never get the fence to stand up all round. It always lies down at the sides.

There's a garden at the front, and a garden at the back. They're both big, but the one at the back is *really* big. We're going to put a form there, and a table, and have tea out there! And next to it – no, next but one – there's a field, with a horse in it called Dolly. And I've got a room of my own! It has lilac wallpaper, with a pattern like curling ribbons on Whitsun hats. And there's a firescreen in front of the fire, a mirror screen.

I explored today. I went on a long walk. Up Leicester Road and in and out of the side-streets. It's called Broughton Park, but it isn't a park, it's houses. They're really posh houses. Shapes I've never seen before, I didn't know houses could be shaped however you like. And it's a really magic place because they don't have numbers, they have names! The houses have names! Some of the names are Ray-Lou or Davera or Sydesta. It's a bit like a *Manchester Guardian* crossword puzzle. I've never seen that before . . . like linking arms when you walk down the street. You'd have to find someone with a name that fits together with yours to make a nice sound, and marry them. But one is different. A house called Interlude. Interlude . . . It sounds very calm, very peaceful, very quiet, like the time between day and night when there is only one star and everything is turning blue. I have been saying it to myself all evening. Interlude . . .

Daddy is making the window-panes into little diamonds.

There's a tent in next door's back garden. And two boys.

The Cowan twins next door invited me to play in their tent. You have to crawl in. They got me to crawl in front of them, and then they smacked me on the bottom – not really hard, just to see what it was like, I think – and said 'Take it like a man.'

You have to have so many pairs of shoes to go to the Manchester High School. Outdoor shoes, indoor shoes, gym shoes. They don't have laces. They have elastic fronts. I've never seen shoes like that before.

I like to go in the cloth-shops along Bury New Road, when Mammy is choosing something. Tussore silk, Macclesfield silk, shantung silk, taffeta, satin, crêpe de Chine . . . I can tell them all. And serge, and corduroy, and velvet, and gaberdine, and twill, and drill, and calico, and muslin, and gingham, and petersham, and nun's veiling . . . I love the slaps and the thuds and the whacks the stuff makes when Mr Feingold rolls it over and over on the counter before he measures it.

★

Art silk doesn't mean what I thought it meant. I thought it meant something very beautiful that people make to be joyful. But it means artificial. You can call it rayon.

Mammy's making my gym slip. I hope it will be the same as the other people's. I think you're supposed to get bought ones. She's making a four-and-a-half-inch hem for letting down.

'Stuff' is really cloth. 'Cloth' is the proper word, not 'stuff'. Or you can say 'material'. But I think 'material' means other things as well . . . I'm not quite sure what.

Auntie Gertie's frock is black satin, and very tight. It has beads all over it, like caraway seeds blinking. She is going to a wedding, but she says she has just got time to clean the herrings. The scales fly up like puddle-spray all over her satin sleeves and her satin front that bulges out, but she doesn't care. She doesn't put on an apron, or even push her sleeves up. They are very tight and she would have to undo them at her wrists.

'Tell Simie, chuckie, the wheelchair needs mending. He should come and see it.' She washes her hands, and goes.

Simie is Daddy. His name is Simon really. Auntie Gertie is his cousin, not really my auntie at all. She is very big and fat, but not at all quivery.

Will I be able to tell him? He hates me.

In the next room Uncle Joe is pressing things. I can hear the iron thumping down, and the hiss when he spits on it. I was sent. I go out again very quietly so that he doesn't hear me.

I don't know how old Shim is. Perhaps he is as old as Ellie. Perhaps even older. He is always in a wheelchair, so you can't tell, and his back is humped over. His friends come and push him to football matches, or to Charlie Chaplin on the croft. Sometimes they lift him up and carry him between them. He is very heavy.

Once I had been sent there, and they all came back from a football match, and Auntie Gertie had made kichlech, and lokshen pudding, and a huge pile of potato blintzes, and spread it all out on the table for them, and they laughed and joked, and lifted Shim out on to a chair. They are always laughing and joking and talking together.

Ginger Goldman is one of them. He is very tall, and thin and bony, with very red hair like Daddy's moustache, and freckles all over his face like the dust from a tulip. Sometimes when Mammy has tulips on the table because visitors are coming, the golden dust sprinkles out on the white cloth and leaves a yellow stain, yellower than Ginger Goldman's freckles, which are brownish.

They all say hello to me. Nothing else.

I have to have a tie. Like Grammar School boys. And a blazer for the summer. And a gabardine raincoat. And we've had to *order* my hat because when they measured my head it was so big. Seven-and-three-eighths. Or was it seven-and-seven-eighths? Everything's black and gold.

And the list of books! We're trying to get them all second-hand. I love it – getting all these books second-hand, in those holes in the wall in the Shambles and all the streets round the Cathedral . . . Shudehill, and Withy Grove, and Hanging Ditch . . .

I like breathing on the table and polishing off my breath. It's like suddenly understanding something.

I was rubbing up the knives for Mammy on the slopstone when I heard Auntie Ettie say 'I thought you were so good, Annie. The way you didn't cry.' Then Mammy said 'I told her it was no use coming.'

They were at the other end of the kitchen, with the *Manchester Guardian* spread out on the table, looking at a picture.

When they had gone, I went and looked at it. It said underneath, 'Miss Hannah Raphael.' It said she had been headmistress at the Manchester Jews' School for a very long time. 'Stalwart educationist.' Like stalwart knight.

*

Auntie Ettie is rather fat, but quivery, and she is kind. Daddy says she is M.D.

Today I went to the Rialto and I saw a picture about a man and his little girl, who live on a houseboat. He keeps beating her, because she visits people who are kind to her. He takes off his belt, unbuckling it slowly – all you see are his hands undoing his belt and he beats her with it.

A barge, not a houseboat.

If I lie in front of the firescreen in my room, with my knickers off and my knees up and spread out, I can see what I'm actually like. Like tangerine slices.

I make friends with Dolly every day. I stand right up against the fence and she comes up to me.

The shape of my lips is changing. I look in the mirror every day. The old shape is outside, a rim, like a pink shadow. Everyone must see it. It frightens me. Will it go on like this? Why does nobody say anything?

> Lord behold us with thy blessing
> Once again assembled here . . .

We sang this on the first morning. It's like *Fifth Form At St Dominic's*. I wondered if it would be like this. It made me shiver, to be like books.

I lie in front of the firescreen often, looking at myself. It's so good in this house. Having a room of my own, and a firescreen. It's funny that you don't know what you're like, if you don't have a firescreen.

    But what is it called? Isn't there a word for it, like elbow and knee and ankle?

★

What's The Change? Women go M.D. after The Change . . . ?
I heard Daddy say so. Nobody ever tells you anything.

Mammy has got me *The Holiday Annual* for getting the scholarship. She asked what I wanted and I said that. I really knew
it would make her sad, and that she really wanted me to say
something hard so that she'd be proud of me. But I did want
that. And she got it.
    It's the annual of the *Magnet* and the *Gem* and the *Popular*.
Perhaps she didn't know. But she must have been sad when she
looked at it. I love it. I read it all the time.

I love the way Dolly dances round the edge of the field as if she's
playing games with the wind and you can't see it. But it frightens me a bit too. When she's just near my hand and she tosses her
head and snorts, it makes me jump.

A lot of the girls come by train, from Irlam and Urmston. Even
Alderley Edge. Even Marple. Ones like Patricia, and Daisy. And
some of the girls didn't get scholarships. They've been here since
they were seven, and they pay. And some of them *board*. What's
that? Is it like a boarding-house, like Mrs Butterworth's or Mrs
Ramsay's? It can't be, because that's for holidays. I think it's
something very posh.

My lips are still changing.

We have a form mistress. She is supposed to look after you. Her
name is Miss Callinan. She says 'Gels'. She says 'Noo-ga'. She
claps her hands and says 'This room is like a bear-garden.'

Miss Treloar says 'Of course we all know there are some people who have a bath once a week.' It stays in my mind in a
funny way like a tickle in your ear. Does she mean something?

We have a bath in our new house. We don't go to the public

baths. We have a bath and a basin in my room, for everyone. My mother calls it The Toilet Room, but I call it my bedroom because my bed's there, and that's what it is really. I always have a bath once a week because our bath is right inside the house. Does she mean something?

I heard Daddy say that when Cecil Cohen was little he called the kerbstone the mantlepiece, and that means he's M.D. And he said Mrs Cohen liked to hear him say it, so she is M.D. as well.

But the kerbstone *is* the same shape as the mantlepiece, and I think it was clever of Cecil when he was little to see that. And I'm glad Mrs Cohen liked him to say it.

He often says Mammy's friends – or relations – are M.D. The women, I mean.

Yesterday was a bit awful. I bought Dolly an apple. I've read about how you have to keep your hand flat like a plate and put the apple on it. I climbed the fence, and that's what I did. But when she'd eaten the apple, she pushed her nose into my pocket, and under my arm, and into my face, and I began to get frightened, and to run, and she chased me right round the field, and I had to climb the fence very quickly. I'm not quite used to horses yet.

I went to the Rialto to see *Beau Geste*. When he died his brother put his body on the Viking ship, and they set it on fire and it moved out to sea in flames, trailing gold, burnishing the waves. Ronald Coleman was Beau.

Ellie says the Manchester Grammar School is much older than our school because it was founded in 1515 and there wasn't even one girls' school then, and it's much bigger too, and they sing *Forty Years On* as well as *Lord Behold Us*. I wish we did. It's in Ellie's School Songbook for Boys, and I know it by heart. It has that same holy feeling as *Lord Behold Us*, but sadder still, and the end bit, 'Follow up . . .' I think is to do with hunting foxes, I'm not sure . . . it sounds like a hunting horn, as if it's cruel as well as holy and beautiful.

I told him we were learning Latin from the very first week, and he says that's nothing, he's learning Greek too. Well, I will be later.

I'm glad I always read the *Magnet* and the *Gem* and the *Popular.* I already know bits of Latin.

I've got a picture postcard of Gladys Cooper. She is so beautiful.

My mouth is still changing . . . It's moving . . . Nobody says anything.

If I go to Jane Feingold's on Shabbos, I mustn't ring the bell. I have to kick and kick at the door. If God didn't want people to work and get tired on the Sabbath Day, he certainly wouldn't have meant them to kick and kick at a door. I should have thought he'd want them to ring the bell, like we do at our house.

Jane lives in Wellington Street. She's in my form at school. She got a scholarship too, but not from Derby Street. From Waterloo Road, I think.

When you say to Jane Feingold's mother 'How are you?' she tells you. For ages. I never knew anyone did that.

I've been to Crumpsall library! You go right up Leicester Road. I've never seen so many books, and you can touch each one, take them off the shelf, read bits, put them back, read another! You can stay there for *hours.* But I suppose you have to pretend you're choosing, not just reading, so it's best not to stay too long. There's a thick white rope across, to divide the children's part from the grown-ups' part, but I can duck under it.

★

91

When I was walking to Heaton Park, I saw an Armstrong Sidney. *Sidd-e-ley*. I know it was an Armstrong Siddeley because there was a sphinx on the bonnet, like on the cigarette cards.

Jane was cutting her fingernails when I went round this afternoon. She put them all very carefully in a screw of paper, and burnt them on the fire. She said you have to. She said it's very important not to let anyone find a bit of fingernail, or they would have power over you. She said it's in the Bible. I said it isn't.

We've got a telephone. It's like a daffodil, but black.

Daddy keeps saying 'God save me from an intelligent woman!' Sort of saying it to himself so that Mammy can't say anything, but wanting her to hear.

If Mammy and Daddy have gone to Mr and Mrs Galansky's or Mr and Mrs Cohen's or the Rusholme Theatre, I have to answer it. I have to get the name and the address and the message. It's very hard to hear and to copy it down before they go away, and I don't like asking a grown-up to keep saying it again because they'll get angry. But I'm afraid someone might die if I don't, and I'm responsible.

When it rings, I jump, even if I'm just near it, and can see it. I'd sooner be in another room and have to walk to it through the ringing (like a cat shouting for food even when you're bringing it).

When I give Daddy the messages, he will stare at me with his black face, hating me. But I *have* to give him them.

Bobbie Goller is in the room upstairs. I haven't seen her for a long time. Nobody has said anything. I don't know how she got there.

At breakfast, my father is shouting to my mother that he carried her there in his arms, like a child.

*

When she bangs on the floor with a stick, I have to go up.

Whenever I am in the room downstairs, when we are all having something to eat, I am afraid a bang will come. I am always expecting it, but I jump, as if it surprises me.

Her hand is like a witch's hand. Or like a bat, holding on to the bedclothes. I have seen pictures of bats.

Her nose, and the place where her eyes are, shine out white like a mask. But she is not wearing a mask. I don't think she is wearing a mask.

She has never spoken to me. Now she says one word. 'Water!' She throws it at me like a stone, hard. She hits me with it.

I give her the special cup that is shaped like a teapot. My hand is trembling. She puts her hand out, and holds it. Her hand is trembling too.

When I go, I have to leave the stick near her hand, so that she can bang again.

I come down, and they are quarrelling, sending their words slithering under the door like hissing snakes, like Phoebe.

Today I pass the room upstairs. The door is a little bit open. I can see my father. He is sitting behind Bobbie Goller's head, and she is a skeleton like in the Myths and Legends. And he is combing her long white hair, combing and combing.

Rapunzel, Rapunzel, let down your hair.

Now the room upstairs is empty.

And no one has said anything.

We do Latin. Mr Quelch in the *Magnet* teaches Latin. Amo,

amas, that means I love. And the boys are laughing all the time, and pinching Billy Bunter. But here it is about wars and shields and swords and how many soldiers are dead.

Noo-ga is nougat. I never heard anyone say that before.

We have desks that open up, and you put your books inside them.

Miss Callinan says I'm a disgrace to the school because my hair sticks out. I can't help the way it is. It used to be soft and wavy, but now it's fuzzy and frizzy. Like a bush. If I put a slide in it and manage to fasten it, it pops open again. Even a very large one does. I break a comb on it practically every day.

Miss Callinan keeps giving me order marks and saying I'm letting down the form. If she didn't give me order marks, I wouldn't be, but she has to. I can't help it. It frightens me, because it's changing. Like my mouth is changing. I don't know why this is happening.

There's going to be a Fancy Dress Party at school. I've never been to one but I've read about them in books.

Mammy is going to make me a fancy dress costume on the sewing machine. She's going to get a pattern.

She says I'm going as a letter-box.

Books are so heavy to carry home each day for homework. I have a brown attaché case. A-tatch-er case. It looks like leather, but it's cardboard really.

Mammy says she will have the letter-box finished in time. It will go over my head.

Vera Cohen's hair is red, but a different red from mine. My

father has a red moustache. And all his cousins, like Ginger Goldman, have red hair. And my mother's name used to be Cohen too, before she married my father. So I said to her, to Vera Cohen, 'Perhaps we're cousins.' She looked a bit surprised.

So I said 'Have you got an Auntie Ettie?' And she thought a bit, and then she said 'Yes.'

Yesterday I said to Vera Cohen, 'Have you got an Uncle Percy?' She said 'Yes.' So I said 'Does he wear glasses?' And she said he did!

This afternoon I said 'Was your Uncle Percy a soldier once?' So she said he was! And then I said 'Was it in Egypt?' and she said it was!

It's like sherbet sweets, when they fizz in your mouth!

Vera Cohen is so *stupid!* She said today she didn't really have any of those aunties and uncles, and she's not one of my family! She's *so stupid!* She doesn't understand anything! She can't even pretend!

I don't even like her anyway! I don't even want her in my family!

I went to the Fancy Dress Party. Everybody was dressed as shepherdesses and princesses and fairy godmothers. Everyone looked beautiful. I was the only letter-box.

I don't think their mothers made those costumes on the sewing machine. I don't think you're meant to do that. I think there's a place where you get them. How do people know?

I don't think anyone has ever come to a Fancy Dress Party as a letter-box before . . . But they must have done, or there wouldn't be patterns . . . would there?

If you run fast right across the school playground, you run into the railings, and your body stops but your foot goes underneath, and the metal scrapes it and it bleeds. I try to do this every day.

95

It hurts quite a bit. If it bleeds into my black school stockings, will I get blood poisoning?

When everyone is out and I have to answer the telephone, I read the books in Daddy's bookcase. The very big one in the surgery. It takes up a whole wall. There are hundreds of books in it. *Classic Myths and Legends . . . Celtic Myths and Legends . . . Indian Myths and Legends . . . Myths and Legends of Babylonia and Assyria . . .*

I like the stories about Orpheus. When he played his lyre, wild beasts would come softly out of the forest and stand bewitched.

I read them again last night. Even the rivers would stand still and listen.

On the wall in the surgery is a picture of a little girl with nothing on. She has taken off her red cloak and dropped it on the floor, and her bottom is lit up, and round and rosy in the firelight. And you can see she's going to get into the big bed where there's a wolf dressed up in a nightgown. I think it's Little Red Ridinghood, but there's nothing in the one I know about getting into bed with the wolf. This morning I asked Mammy about it. She said in some stories she does. She didn't want to talk about it very much. Grown-ups never do want to talk about things you're interested in. They don't like you being interested in anything. And then they say 'Why aren't you *interested* in anything?'
I don't like this picture. I don't know why exactly.

I think children's bottoms don't belong to children; they belong to grown-ups.

In another book, about illnesses, there's a picture of a parrot. No, a cockatoo. At least, I think it is a cockatoo. It has a sort of crest on its head. I can't quite make it out.

★

In one of the *Myths and Legends* books, there's the story of Roland and Charlemagne. It has a picture of a knight kneeling with his head bent down, and the back of his neck bared, waiting. He is waiting, gracefully, for the sword to cut his head off. You can feel he is doing it *with love*. Is that what love is?

I go to Eva's a lot. I must find another family than my own, and Wellington Street's easy to walk to. There are three girls. There's Ray, who's older than Eva, and Esther who's the oldest. She's working. And there's Eva of course. She's the same age as me. They're always talking together, and they make room for me. I mean, make room for me in their talking.

It takes at least an hour to walk to school. Bury New Road, past Victoria Station and the Cathedral, down Cross Street and over Albert Square, and into Oxford Road. I go different ways different days. If I look in Sherratt and Hughes' window it takes an hour and a half, but I only do that on the way home. Sometimes I go in, and read a book. If an assistant comes up to me I close it and say 'I'm afraid that's not quite what I'm looking for.' I stay in the shop for a little bit after that, very calmly, turning over one or two more books but not opening them, and then walk out *slowly*.

You have to pay a penny a day for a space at the dinner table if you bring sandwiches. Miss Tiano sits on a sort of stage at her own table. She has to keep order. She dips her spoon in her plate, and raises her eyes, and doesn't know where to look. Everyone stares at her.

Doctors are always pressing you somewhere, and saying 'Tell me if it hurts'. But they can't make me.

It happened again, at the examination. The doctor kept saying 'Tell me if it hurts', and when I wouldn't say it did, he kept on and on, trying to make me. And when I still wouldn't say, I think he began to get cross . . . not pleased.

I don't understand.

The people who report you because they saw you in town without your school stockings on, or without your hat, or you're chewing in the street, and then it's read out at morning assembly — they're complete strangers! How can grown-ups behave like that! It's like a conspiracy. People getting together. Against children.

Is that why we have so many bits of uniform?

If you take off your stockings, or your hat, you've still got the black blazer on, or the black raincoat. And people who don't know you and can't mind their own business report you.

All the same, I *like* wearing the blazer. And I like having the school badge on the pocket in gold, and belonging, like people do in books.

Not the hat, though. The elastic hurts my ears.

Afraid the World is Falling

1929–1931

Eva has a brother too, but I've never seen him. He's called Joe. He's at University, because he's the boy.

Esther and Ray have to learn girls' things, even though they all got scholarships to Dover Street. Their Dad has a workshop, a little factory that makes caps, with about twenty girls working there who call him 'Dad', and Esther types the letters and does the accounts. That's the bills and the pay packets and things. And Ray does Home Economics at school, and typing too. I don't think she really wants to. Ray is always making jokes about people, and laughing.

You can say Dover Street. But really it's the Manchester High School.

People at school think that if someone is doing Home Economics instead of Latin, then they're stupid. But they can't be stupid if they got a scholarship, can they?

I've never seen Joe. He's never there. Even when it's holiday-time, he isn't there.

*

But sometimes when I go to Eva's, he must be there, he must be lying in bed or something, because they're all busy doing something for him, like polishing his boots, or ironing his shirt, as if they think he's wonderful, and mustn't get his hands dirty, or get tired.

I don't know how it is, but somehow they tell you secretly that he's too stupid to do it for himself. Secretly, like as if they were winking at you.

I mean, without saying it. But they *have* to polish his shoes, and iron his shirt, and mend his socks, and look after him. And they do.

Uncle Larry comes from Dublin. He was a chazan at the shool there. He has a soft and gentle Irish voice. Daddy said to Uncle Percy that he's creepy. They have a little piano – no, Mammy says an American organ – in their front room. Sometimes he will give a sort of concert and sing *Meyer My Girl*, or *The Mountains of Mourne*.

> *Twas on an April eve*
> *That I first met her,*
> *Many an eve shall pass*
> *Ere I forget her . . .*

> *Dwells she in beauty there,*
> *Meyer my girl . . .*

It's *Maire*. I've seen it on the music. But you say Meyer, like Meyer's shop.

I wish I could do gym.

Climbing up the ropes, one hand after the other, the end of it tucked between your legs. Sliding down again, changing hands in rhythm like a folk-dance, so it doesn't burn.

I love watching Margery Hovell. She does it very beautifully, slipping down, arm after arm, in little waterfalls.

★

In cataract after cataract, to the sea.

But it's an extra. You don't get it with your scholarship.

People always keep trying to open the lavatory door when I'm in, because I'm in such a long time. I'm always constipated. I keep very quiet, I don't want them to know it's me. They bang with their hands on the door. I keep very quiet. In the end they give up and go to another cloakroom, and when I come out ours is empty and everyone's gone to the formroom. Mammy says I should go to the lavatory every day at the same time. But there isn't *time!* And I can't go just because I'm supposed to!

Church bells ringing, staggering, balancing, reeling, tottering, falling or nearly falling, like a giant, drunk in Hilton Street.
    I don't walk near. I am afraid the world is falling.

He's started to tell my mother how to cook. She's been cooking for years! She was probably cooking when she was a child. And he starts ordering her about in the kitchen, telling her to make smart things like soufflés. I couldn't bear it. Suddenly I was very angry and I said 'First she has to stop teaching because she's married to you, when teaching is what she cares about, and now you won't even let her do what she's allowed to do, in the kitchen!' He was very startled.
    She was too.
    I was glad.

Everyone is out again. I read the stories of the knight whose name is Death. A noble knight rides through the deep, dark forests. He meets another knight who raises his visor, and underneath is not his face, but a skull. I freeze, but I can't stop reading them.

Yesterday I got trapped in the room with Mammy and Daddy. And Mammy flung up the window and screamed 'Murder! He's going to murder me!' And then they saw me. Whenever something like that happens, I can't move, and I can't speak.

That cockatoo is in very ugly colours. All the pictures in that illness book are in ugly colours. Colours like that aren't for looking at. They make your back shiver like screeching chalk.

My father leaves the medicines on the table for me to deliver. They are wrapped in beautiful white paper, brilliant and shining, and perfectly creased like the pleats in my gym slip that have just been pressed. And they are fastened with one bright red splash of sealing wax. I don't mean a splodge. It is like a Ludo counter, perfectly round and smooth. Where does he get that white shiny paper? I have never seen it anywhere else. I can't do anything so neatly. So exquisitely. Exquisitely. That is a good word. I can't even measure lines properly. In geometry, every time I measure the same line I get a different answer. I hate geometry, but I love algebra. Algebra is like writing poems or stories, or thinking of them. Geometry is like my Uncle Simie who gets hold of your wrist so that you can't get away.

But the medicine packets are very beautiful, like my bandage was.

The Last Watch of Hero. Leander . . . *Le-ander* . . . On the surgery wall. Every night Hero lit a lamp to guide Leander through the waves. But one night there was a storm, and the waves tossed him and hurled him, till he could scarcely breathe, and the wind blew out the guiding light, and he drowned. Hero waited by the window, waited and waited. And when she realised he had drowned, she threw herself into the waves, and died too.

I've seen that picture in the art gallery in town. Her eyes are red with crying. Or perhaps it's with staring through the night. No, it's crying, because they're wet, and staring makes them dry . . .

He stands in front of *The Last Watch of Hero*, and talks about it as if he had painted it himself. But I don't think he did.

It is often hard to tell with him. But I don't think he did.

Though I am not absolutely sure.

I've been reading one of Sleena's library books. The mother in it hits the little girl with her shoe. She makes her lie on the bed on her front, and then she hits her with the heel part. She keeps doing it.

Sleena does the fires for the Feingolds. She lives with them. They call her 'the girl'. Everyone who has someone to help them says 'the girl'. But actually she's grown-up. She's lots older than Esther. Maybe as old as their mother. I think I'm the only one who says 'Sleena'.

They all of them, Eva and Ray and Esther and Sleena and Mrs Feingold, they shout and argue and call each other names at the top of their voice, and are quite happy.

It's Selena, not Sleena. Se-le-na.

Selena reads novels. She lends them to Jane and to Ray and Esther, and they lend them to me.

They're kept in the chest of drawers, in a big deep drawer, because the Feingolds are very frum, and only religious books and textbooks are on the shelves, and anyway they're supposed to be wicked.

The drawer isn't locked or anything. I don't know whether it's because the men are all so silly that they don't think of looking in the drawer, or whether it's because they think women and girls are just not worth bothering about. But none of the men ever take a novel out and rip it up and throw it out of the window. So how do we *know* they think they're wicked and evil? But we *do* know.

★

Ellie has a bicycle. Daddy said girls shouldn't ride bicycles. He said it ruins the shape of the pelvis.

I don't know why there's a picture of a cockatoo in a book about people's illnesses. Unless you get it off cockatoos, and the picture is to show you what to watch out for in case they're flying around. I can't understand the words. They're medical words.

I have to clear up Daddy's dispensary every week. He's built it in his surgery room out of wood – a bit like a succa, but not pretty – no palms or fruit hanging down.

There are pills and tablets and powders and liquids scattered all over the shelves and the floor, the colours trodden like hopscotch chalk, very beautiful. The pills roll along the shelves as though they are desperately trying to escape and the tablets balance on their edges and rock backwards and forwards. If they're trodden together I have to sweep them up and throw them away. But I try to save them. I try to pick them up and put them back in their right bottles. But I don't really know where they go. How can I know? Daddy never speaks to me.

It is as if a storm has rushed in, turned everything over, and rushed out again.

Mammy says she won't do it. Her voice goes very hard as if it's locked up.

The colours are beautiful. It is like Aladdin's Cave. But I have to clear it up, and put things back where they should be, and I don't know where.

I think something is happening about Uncle Izak and Sybil Thorndike. I am never quite sure if something is *really* happening, because nobody says anything. Or they start, and stop when I come into the room.

It is true. It is in the *Manchester Guardian.* Sybil Thorndike is going to be in a play of Uncle Izak's. It is that book he wrote called *The Five Books of Mr Moses*. It is about a man and his daughter.

They love each other very much, but she marries a Christian, so he says she is dead, and he will never speak of her again. Sybil Thorndike says it is wonderful and she will be in it.

My father was talking to Mr Galansky, and I heard him say Queenie's name. He said when he was at their house, Queenie's father had called up the stairs for Queenie to fetch him something, and there was no answer. And my father said to Mr Galansky 'Dirty little bitch!' He said of course she was in. She just didn't want to come. She was making a fool of her father, he said.

Is it wicked for a girl not to come running like a little dog?

I think of Queen Vashti who didn't come when King Ahasueros called her to show her off to his courtiers. And he banished her from his court.

The way my father was talking, I don't think Queenie's father minded. I think he just went and got it for himself.

The *Manchester Guardian* says Sybil Thorndike is coming next week to start rehearsing Uncle Izak's play.

The medicines are always for people in Broughton Park, where the houses have names. The sealing wax is like a drop of blood on a white tablecloth.

I read a book, where geranium petals fell on the table and reminded the woman in the story of bloodstains on a man's white shirt. It kept repeating – 'bloodstains on a man's white shirt'. It was one of Selena's library books. All the Feingold girls read it, and then I did.

The *Manchester Guardian* says Uncle Izak and Sybil Thorndike have quarrelled, about the way the play should be. My father told Uncle Percy that Uncle Izak is a B.F. 'always interfering'. B.F. means Bloody Fool. But you can say Bally Fool without B.F.

Annie Binder's sister has run away to Paris to be an artist. And I think to call herself Polly, because she hates Pearl. And to have an Eton Crop too. The grown-ups are talking about it.

Annie Binder is one of Mammy's friends. They are both called Annie. Her voice is very soft, and her hair is done like a little girl's.

They are not going to do the play after all. The *Manchester Guardian* says the theatre people are going back to London because Uncle Izak won't stop arguing.

This afternoon Mammy had visitors. There was seed cake, not cherry cake which I love. I don't like seed cake. It smells strange, and looks strange. The seeds are long and thin, with slots in them, like nearly-closed eyes . . . Slots or slits . . . Caraway, they are called. That is the best thing about them. Caraway, caraway.

Annie Binder had brought a letter from her sister, and she read it out loud to everyone.

'Dear good little sister Anne.' I didn't hear the rest, because Mammy sent me to get some more hot water.

What is a blue-stocking?

When I came back, and I was at the slit of the door, the grown-ups were all chirping together. The sound was like sparrows in the road, when the cartwheels have flattened out the horse-muck, and they are all pecking at it. And I heard Annie Binder suddenly say 'Are you ever sorry now, Annie?' And all the chirruping stopped, because they were listening for Mammy's answer. And she said slowly, 'No . . . I would have been called a blue-stocking . . . No one would ever have spoken to me.'

. . . What *is* a blue-stocking?

My father says I am invited to Vivie Hytner's birthday party. I don't know why. I don't even know her.

There's a house on the way to Heaton Park that is not like other houses. It is very low and long and wandering and, somehow, kind.

Serene. Serene. That's what it is. It makes me think of the day Eta did Number Two on the sofa and Eta's mother didn't shout at all, but just looked at her kindly. *Serenely.* And there are statues in the garden. I've looked at them through the gate. I have never seen a house and garden like that before. It is like a magic island that isn't always there. Though I think this house *is* always there. But how can you tell? Perhaps it is only there on the days when I walk past it.

I don't understand about that house. Who lives there?

Today I was clearing up the dispensary shelves when I came across something as lovely as a spiral shell. It is a little elf curled up in a bottle. I looked at it for a long time. A very long time. I think I love it more than anyone I know. It is really dear to me.

Mrs Hytner is one of my father's smart patients. He has smart patients now. They generally have to do with films – but not *being* in them. He doesn't have the panel ones we had in Fenney Street. And he doesn't go to see ill people in Ancoats any more. He said his Ancoats patients were sewn into their combinations. He says Vivie Hytner is one year younger than me, and Judith her sister is two years older.

My mother says I am going to wear one of the frocks from the box that came from London. I have two cousins, Minnie and Lilian, who live in London where everyone is very smart and talks bay windows, and they send boxes of clothes they've grown out of.

There's a frock of Lilian's in it, a party frock, like people wear when they're bridesmaid. It is crimson taffeta. The skirt comes down like the petals of a flower, with crimson velvet coming down the middle of each petal. It is a very beautiful dress when it isn't on anybody. Perhaps it was beautiful on Lilian.

The colour makes me very white as if I'm going to drop down dead, because Lilian has black hair and I haven't. And because of the petals you can't turn up the hem like you can ordinary frocks.

My mother puts it on me, and she shouts at me because it makes me look ill, and I should look different. Then she gets some rouge. I don't know where she's got it from. I think my father must have made her get it. He's getting to like smart people.

It was horrible. She dabbed it on my face, and she shouted at me again, because she didn't know how to do it and I didn't look right, and she dabbed on some more, *scrubbed* it on as if she was rubbing a smut off my face with a hanky. I felt terrible. I think she was frightened.

I had to cross Leicester Road so that I could turn the corner and walk along the side of Mandley Park. I had the address in my sock. When I crossed the road, a tramcar was coming along, and an old man with a long white beard got off at the tram-stop and a motorcar didn't stop and knocked him down. I was nearly on the other side of the road by then, nearly at the park, but I saw it all happen as I crossed.

I didn't know what to do. I was supposed to be going to a party, and now an old man had been knocked down and killed. I didn't know what to do. I've never been at a party. This is my first one. I thought I would hear people shouting and crying, and crowds coming and an ambulance ringing, and the tram stuck there, but when I looked round there was no one there and the tramcar had gone on. In the end, I went on too, but I kept thinking of the dead old man, and how I mustn't tell anyone, because I shouldn't be at the party because of the old man being killed. But I didn't know whether I ought to go home or not.

At the party I didn't speak to anyone, and nobody spoke to me. I didn't know anyone. They were all very smart people.

They played blind-man's buff, and I watched. You tie a scarf round someone's eyes so she can't see, and you turn her round fast so that she doesn't know where she is, and you push her so that she nearly falls over, passing her from one to the other and pushing her different ways and laughing, all laughing, and under her blinded eyes you can see her mouth and it sort of smiles as if she hopes someone will stop people hurting her. It's horrible. Is this what parties are like?

Whenever I could, I looked at Vivie Hytner. I have never seen anyone so beautiful. I looked at her all the time. She had a flame-coloured frock on, and her cheeks and her lips were flame-coloured too. And her hair was black, deep black and shining. I didn't want to do anything but look at her from the time I came till it was time to go.

When I walked home, I was afraid to be back in Leicester Road. I thought there would be crowds on the pavement talking about the old man, and blood on the road. But there was no one. And nothing. I don't understand.

My father asked me who was at the party, but I couldn't tell him, and he was angry. And still nobody has talked about the old man. I looked in the paper, but there was nothing. Nobody has said anything.

Selena got *Hatter's Castle* out of the library, and she is letting us read it.

When she pushed Ray's sleeve up off her wrist so she didn't get it wet when she was washing up, something flashed inside me, frightening me.

I am excited now when I go to clear up the dispensary. Because among all the colour flung about is that tiny person in the bottle.

So dainty. So quiet and still in the middle of all that riotous colour. Riotous . . . Is that a word?

Excited and sad. That's how loving is.

I keep thinking about the old man. Why doesn't anyone say anything? Why isn't there anything in the *Manchester Guardian*?

Ellie is teaching Queenie and me to play bridge. He learned it in Cambridge. Important people don't play whist, he says.

I am still reading *Hatter's Castle*. I can't stop reading it, although it makes me want to scream, but I don't know how to scream.

Her father has power over everyone's life. He owns everyone. Her mother, her sister, her brother, Nessie . . . I once read a story about a ceiling that kept coming down, lower and lower, on everyone's head, crushing them to death, and there was no way to escape it. That's how I feel when I read *Hatter's Castle*, that it is coming down lower and lower on my head. But every night I read a bit more.

I have finished *Hatter's Castle*. Nessie hanged herself because she didn't get the scholarship. She brushed her hair to hang herself, and put on her best clothes that she wore for the scholarship that her father was sure she would get, but she didn't.

Margaret and I play paper cricket on top of the tram. One of us has to be English, the other has to be Australian, and we write down our side – Jardine and Larwood and Conny and Woolley . . . or else Bradman and Macartney and so on . . . And we get out a book from our attaché case, any book, and count ten letters along a line, any line, and if it's *s* it's stumped, and if it's *l* it's l.b.w., and if it's *r* it's run out. *C* is caught. *B* is bowled, of course. All the letters in between are runs, and you count how many. The pages of my schoolbooks are covered with dots where

I counted with my pencil. I like Margaret a lot. We laugh at the same things.

I saw a magazine the other day – I think it was *Punch* but perhaps it was the *Humourist* – and it had a whole page of Test cricketers' signatures. Bradman and Larwood and Oldfield and Ponsford and Woodfall and Jardine. I can't remember how many others. And each signature made that person's face! That person's nose, that person's eyes, and forehead, and chin, and hair! I'll cut it out, to keep. It's so clever and funny.

We're in St Anne's! At Mrs Ramsay's, there's a piano in the front room, and somebody sits down and plays and everyone else stands round it and sings. There's always piles of music in the music-stool, and when there's no one else in the front room I pick out the tunes with one finger.

Sometimes I wish I'd said the piano instead of the violin. It would make harmony lessons much easier. And I'd love to play with people singing around me. But I know I was supposed to do the hard one.

Charmaine, my Charmaine . . .

> *I wonder why you keep me waiting,*
> *Charmaine, my Charmaine.*
> *I wonder when bluebirds are mating*
> *Will you come back again? . . .*

Carolina Moon . . . Car-o-li-na Moon . . . That's like climbing a four-bar gate, sitting on the top, and jumping down the other side.

But sad, when you sing it.

> *Carolina Moon, keep shining,*
> *Shining on the one who waits for me.*

★

This one looks very new. Ha-*a*ppy days are he-*e*re again . . . There's a bar-line right in the middle each time. Ha-*a*ppy days are he-*e*re again . . . Ha-*a*ppy days are he-*e*re again . . . It's very difficult. You have to think so hard. You can't ever stop thinking.

Last night we went to Blackpool to see the Illuminations. Blackpool hurts my ears, but the Illuminated Tram is like Aladdin's Cave, jewels raining down as if they were pouring through someone's fingers.

Round the piano, someone lifted up the Spanish shawl that covered the top, and something flashed across my eyes, frightening me . . .

Outside all the shops, mixed up with the buckets and spades and the windmills and water-wings there are stands with picture postcards on them of children with a bare bottom and a bright red hand-print on it where a grown-up has smacked really hard so that every finger and thumb shows, and the child is crying. And grown-ups pick them up and laugh and show them to each other.

The little elf in the bottle has gone. And I loved it. It was my friend.

Plates of Gold

1931–1932

There's a boy living near us who goes to the Manchester Grammar. He is big. Not just old, I don't mean, but big. Big like a man.

I think he probably looks bigger than he is because he has a school cap on. If I see him in Leicester Road, I always walk just behind him. And when he goes down a turning I follow him.

Sometimes he gets on the same bus as I do, from Town. Then I stay on one stop past my own stop, and get off behind him. Then I walk back home again.

Really, I think he's boring. But following him is exciting. Like a spy. And I have to do it.

Walking in the rain, through Fennel Street and Long Millgate, Cateaton Street, the Old Shambles, Hanging Ditch, Shudehill, and Withy Grove. Cheese! The smell of cheese!

And then the books! The books! Barrows of them, boxes of them.

Barrows are different from barrels.

But the best are in the caves, under the kerbstone, underground like Peak's Cavern, cramming and clustering and knobling into the walls as if they're part of them – like knobly things that grow out of trees. Here . . . *The Hound of the Baskervilles, Four Feathers, Jeremy and Hamlet, The Scarlet Pimpernel, Three Men in a Boat, The Sign of Four, Berry and Co., Dracula, The Green Hat, Frankenstein, The Three Musketeers, Raffles* . . . like friends who sit round a fire silently, but turn round and smile at you as you come in.

It's lucky I need so much tram fare and bus fare to get to school. Now that I know the way, I can save it all up for concerts and theatres and films and second-hand books, and walk instead.

Today I went into Forsythe's. I go there often now. I said 'I want to choose some Russian folk song records. Could you give me some to listen to, please?' I do this with all sorts of things – records, and books, even pianos once. When I've spent hours listening or reading, I say politely 'I'm sorry, there's nothing here that's quite what I want,' and I go. They always believe me.

The lady whispered to her friend, and together they made up a big pile. The first lady carried it into the listening room for me. She said 'It will be too heavy for you, love.'

I played the top one. It was the *Volga Boat Song*. The other side was *Stenka Razin*. I put on the second one. It was Russian men, singing in Russian. But they were singing the *Strangeways Prison song*! The back of my neck prickled as if there was a ghost behind me, and I was afraid to look round. When it finished, I looked at the label. It said the name in Russian. And then, underneath, in little letters, it said *The Prisoner's Song*. There must be prisoners all over the world, and each one is singing the *Strangeways Prison song* in his own language.

When I said, 'I'm afraid there's nothing that's quite what I want there' my voice was trembly.

★

Selena has got out *The Mighty Atom*. She's going to lend it me when she's finished it.

Queenie faints. Whenever she wants to. I wish I could faint. I can't faint and I can't scream. I don't know how to do it. I have to stay with whatever is happening.

Ellie is in love with Ray Garber. She is the most beautiful girl in the whole of Salford and Manchester. There were peaches in Mrs Topolski's shop-window today, on dark-blue tissue paper cushions, and they were the same velvety colour as Ray Garber's cheeks. Not velvety. Dusty. Or is it dusky?

I'm always walking. I walk for hours. I put on a beret instead of my school hat, and turn up the collar of my black gabardine coat like we're not supposed to have it at school, and I suck in my cheeks as I walk along so that I look like Marlene Dietrich or Greta Garbo.

When I've walked a long way, I often pass men. I always smile at them, and sometimes say 'Good evening.' They are always very friendly and kind.

Yesterday we went to Betws-y-Coed. I think that's how you spell it. There are so many places you can go to if you live in Salford.

Sometimes I think Derbyshire is best of all because the tall mill chimneys and factories are mixed up with the green hills. They stand up like exclamation marks. I think mixing up is the way it should always be. I hate boxing in. Separating.

Selena lent me *The Mighty Atom*. I've been reading it all week-end. It's like *Hatter's Castle*, but a boy this time. He hangs himself because his father makes him study so hard, so that he'll be proud of him.

★

We've been to London! It was Minnie's wedding, and it was in London, and it was in a Palace. Strand Palace. There were lifts everywhere, and carpets. And the plates and cups were gold.

We had eight courses with gold plates. And the last course of all was little round tangerines that opened like petals and inside was orange Sno-fruit like golden snow, crisp and crackling like when you are first out, and your footprints are little lakes of water. It was magic.

Auntie Amelia was frightened of the lift. She had to go back upstairs for her hanky, and she was frightened to go, and she whispered to me, and I went with her and held her hand. Her eyes were quite wild. I don't think she was seeing me. I stayed with her and held her hand going down again.

Everyone says how young Minnie is to get married. She is only six years older than me.

Bobby Jacobs said he was responsible for Ellie and me. He's a year older than Ellie. He's a Rover Scout. I didn't know Jewish people could be Rover Scouts. I thought Scouts were Christian.

He took us on the trains. Tube trains, they're called. We were in a pitchdark tunnel all the time, but when we came into a station, he somehow knew where we were, which I couldn't understand. And the doors opened by themselves, magically – nobody touched them. And they shut again without anyone touching them, but we were on the other side. We'd got out in time.

He gave me a present. Bobby Jacobs did. It said Roger de Gallet on the box, and when I opened it there was paper folded over inside – not newspaper or book paper or tissue paper or silver paper or tracing paper, but a kind of paper I've never seen before, thick and smooth and polished; and it opened like two doors to a banqueting hall. And inside there was a piece of soap, made in an oval shape, with leaves and flowers carved all over it, smelling so beautiful that you closed your eyes; it was like nothing I have ever smelled before, even in flower shops or fruit shops, and a strange and wonderful colour. Not the colour you would expect. Brown. It was brown. It was the colour of the river Irwell, and if it had been chopped off a bar with a rusty kitchen knife that made it all sharp and scratchy, it would have been ugly. But it wasn't. It was a rich, unknown colour, still and mysterious, belonging in Aladdin's cave. And written on it was FOUGÈRE.

Chimborazo, Cotapaxi . . .

It's the first time a boy has given me a present.

Rover Scouts are important, but a bit boring.

Fougère is Fern. I looked it up in Gasc.

Sandalwood, cedarwood, and sweet white wine.

It was orchestra practice last night. I am always late – or almost late – I don't know why this is, when I never stop thinking about getting there early. I always go up to the front of the tram where the guard and the driver are talking together as the tram goes along, and ask them *please* will they go faster because it's my orchestra practice and I'm late. They always look at each other, and then say 'We'll do the best we can for you, love'. They always save me. They're very kind to me. I thank them when I get off.

We're playing *Eine Kleine Nachtmusik*. I love the slow movement.

I am going past the side of Mandley Park, and I can watch the little kids on the swings in the playground. One of them is running across, and a swing hits him right across the head. It is behind me now, but I don't hear anything, nobody screaming or shouting. But it was terrible!

★

It is the next day, and still nobody is talking about it.

Everyone is in the other room, and the door is closed. Mammy is in there, with Uncle Simie and Auntie Essie and Uncle Larry . . . I don't know who else. I don't know what to do. I think Mammy is crying. But nobody tells me anything. I have to do something. I dress up funnily and I go in and dance, to make them laugh.

How can I know Uncle Hymie is dead if they don't tell me? I *know* he is Mammy's favourite brother, but how can I know he is dead! I just wanted her to be happy, that's all, just to be happy. And she's always saying 'You're so shy, and so quiet!' and being angry because I don't join in.

Today I walked a very long way. I talked to a nice man in a cap and an overcoat. And after a while he said 'You shouldn't really be talking to men like this.' He sounded worried, so I smiled at him. I wanted him to know he didn't have to be worried. Then he said, '*I'm* all right, but some men aren't. Some men could do bad things to you.' I could tell he was still worried so I smiled at him again. I didn't say anything at all, just went on. It was kind of him to say that. The men I meet on the street are always very kind. I like smiling at them and having them smile back.

I was walking down Leicester Road with Mammy when I suddenly made up my mind I would tell her something. It was something I'd done, something I felt, that I decided to tell her about. I was really excited to be giving it to her. I hadn't ever done it before. It was like sliding my hand into her hand.

She looked at me in surprise, and didn't say anything for a minute, and then she talked about something else. But I had *given* it to her! It was a present! I will never do it again. She didn't like it! She didn't want it!

Last night I was trying to think if there was any fairytale where no one was cruel, and no one got hurt. And I took *Grimm's*

Fairytales, the big red book, out of the surgery bookcase. And the pages opened by themselves, at *Hansel and Gretel*. I closed it very quickly. I didn't want to see any of the words. I put the book back on the shelf. I need to know exactly where it is . . . that it's *there*. But I don't ever want to see it.

Flashes

1931–1932

Sometimes my father can't use his seat at the Rusholme Theatre because he's been called out, and I go instead. I saw *Hobson's Choice* last night.

I saw *Love on the Dole*. I like watching Wendy Hiller. I like Franklyn Dyall too. If Wendy Hiller was a real person, I mean if she came outside the play, I think she'd be a grown-up you could trust.

This week I saw *See Naples and Die*. There was someone called Curigwen Lewis. I haven't seen her before. She just wandered about the stage with nothing on, and very long hair and a radiant smile. And there were two men who sat at a little table all the time, playing chess and saying nothing, and *they were spies*.

It was a very funny and very lovely play. Curigwen Lewis, with very long hair and that smile. I hope I see her again. And those two funny men.

★

My father talks about Curigwen Lewis and her long hair and her smile. He must have seen her too.

Today, on top of the tram, a man sitting behind me stroked my bottom through the space in the back of the seat. He kept on and on. I kept wriggling away from him, so that he'd stop, but he didn't. And at last I turned round and I said, 'Would you mind *not* doing that.' I said it politely and quietly because he was a grown-up, quite an old one. He looked surprised, and said he was sorry. He was polite too. There were crowds of people on the top, but no one took any notice.

The G string makes me feel I'm going mad. It's the kind with a metal wire coiled round the gut. It *buzzes*, *rattles*, inside the note, somehow, like a frantic dying fly caught on the fly-paper, or even in your hair. I keep looking at people as I play, expecting to see a sort of horror on their faces, but nobody else seems to hear it. It's horrible hearing things that no one else hears.

I've told Mrs Gee about the G string, but she says she can't hear anything. I can't bear playing it. It frightens me.

I went to the Rusholme Theatre again. I like seeing the same people playing different parts. Repertory, it's called.

I've been to Forsythe's and talked to the man about the G string, and he's given me a new one, a different kind. I can't understand why no one else hears it.

When I come in and they're quarrelling, they stop, and there's a frozen silence. Nothing at all, till I go out of the room.
  It's like the black beetles, waiting to move again.

Someone unfastening a belt – a belt on a raincoat, anything –

makes something flash across my eyes . . or across my heart, is it? . . . stopping it for a moment.

There's a song everyone is singing about Betws-y-Coed. People everywhere are singing about Betws-y-Coed like everywhere they are singing the *Strangeways Prison song*.

It is the end of term, and we have to take everything home. Hundreds of books and gym shoes and indoor shoes and my violin. I go very cold when I know the end of term is coming . . . and it is coming for a very long time. Because I'm trying to think how to pack everything in, and I know I can't. Everyone empties their desk and their shoe-locker, and packs their bag or their satchel. And they remind their friends of their address, because they are going to write, or stay with each other. And they say 'The river is at the bottom of our garden.' And then the school is empty. Dark and dusty. No sound. I am left behind, trying to wedge things in, opening and shutting, fastening buckles, and afraid of being locked in the empty school.

I have dreams about losing my violin on the tram, or my attaché case, or my purse, or getting on the wrong tram. When I wake up I don't feel inside my body.

Today I was washing my hands, and Mammy came into the room, and then Daddy came into the room, and they started shouting at each other, and I got between the bath and the wall and I couldn't move any more, and everything went very far away. And I heard Mammy's voice, 'Just look at the child. She's white as a sheet.' She didn't touch me. She was telling him.

Ellie came home – it's the holidays – and I told him how they are always quarrelling and I can't bear it. But he just laughs in that superior way he's got now, and says all parents are like that – they always quarrel. But he doesn't know. He isn't here. He thinks it's nothing!

Ellie says Hamilton Harty was so drunk last night that he fell off his little platform into the Hallé orchestra. But sometimes he says things just to show off.

It's not Betws-y-Coed they're singing about. It's Betty Co-ed. Something quite different. It's something to do with an American college.

It's very strange with words. You have to find your way, like following little white stones on the ground in the night.

I read about the mining disaster in the *Manchester Guardian*. That boy who dashed into all the falling coal . . . 'I'm going with thee, Harry!' That's what he called out to his friend, a grown-up man, following him into the thick black dust and the darkness. No one has seen him since. I don't like to think about him. But I do. I think about him all the time.

Sometimes I am sitting next to someone on the tram, and I can feel her worry and her sadness leaking into me. I move away a little bit, but it leaps over. I think I must have one layer of skin less than everyone else, so that things get in more. Is that possible?

Up in the gods in the Opera House, it's *miles* down to the stage. I always manage to sit almost in the same place. There's a scratch on the wood like a big white spider.

As soon as the doors are opened everyone rushes up the stairs as fast as they can go, *clattering*. It's best really to be in the very top row of all, even though it is so high, because then you can lean your back against the wall, and it doesn't move and it isn't knobbly like knees.

I don't mind standing. I often stand at concerts because there aren't enough forms. But it's good if you can see as well as hear – it's better somehow. I squint under people's arms. And sometimes people push me in front of them, though I never ask.

Evelyn Laye is so beautiful in *Helen*. Pale gold . . . I have been singing that song in my head all day, the one they sing when everyone is telling Paris to get out. Those three notes, like two people pressing as close as they can together . . .

I am trying to get the Beethoven *Romance* right, the double-stopping one. I don't know which I like better, this one or the simple one. I've heard Kreisler playing it on Raymond's gramophone, and he makes it sound like two violins playing together quite lazily and easily, but it's only one violin, and it isn't lazy and easy at all – it's hard.

Dorothy's father is giving me trade-show tickets, though I don't really know him. That's the new pictures that haven't come to the picture-houses yet. When I go to the ordinary pictures, it costs ninepence. But at trade shows I just show the ticket, and go in and sit among all the men, without paying anything. I don't think anybody takes any notice of me. I saw *A Handful of Cloud* yesterday, a gangster picture, sad and beautiful, with Lew Ayres. A handful of cloud is the smoke from a gangster's gun.

So-o-o-o-o-o-o-o-olomon . . .

Oh, I can't sing it like Elisabeth Welch does.

So-o-o-o-o-o-o-o-olomon
Had ten thousand wives.

It's a bit like shool.

Crying Music

1931–1932

I am on holiday in St Anne's with Dorothy and her mother – not with my mother at all. I don't understand why my mother has let me go. She doesn't know Dorothy's mother. She doesn't even know Dorothy. I don't know Dorothy's mother – I think this is the first time I've met her – but I think if my mother met her she would think she was very fast. She thinks all the people who have to do with the film business are very fast – the women, I mean.

I have just discovered that Dorothy's grandmother knew my grandmother – my father's mother, the one who was so silent, and sat secretly combing her long white hair. They were very old friends, from years ago, perhaps from Russia. I didn't think she had a friend, she was so sad and lonely-looking. They must even have talked together . . .

Perhaps that's why they let me go. Perhaps my father said so.

*

I've never been on holiday with a friend before. It's like in a book.

I've got my violin with me – I take it everywhere – and I'm practising the Beethoven *Romances*. Dorothy likes me to do it.

There are two lovely Pierrots in Happy Valley – Algy and Reggie. Algy is the tenor, and Reggie is the baritone. Algy is tall and thin with black hair, and very handsome. Reg is middling height, and fairer. We shared them out. Dorothy had first pick, and got Algy. So I've got Reg. He's squarer-looking, but not really fat.

Today we went into Dorothy's mother's bedroom, because she was out. She generally goes out, and leaves us to do what we want.

We tried all the things on her dressing-table. My mother never has things like that. Dorothy said I wasn't putting the rouge on right. She did it for me. It doesn't go in a dab right in the middle, but nearer to your eyes. When we were ready we went to Happy Valley and sat in the very front row of the pierrot show and stared at Algy and Reg without blinking all the time they were singing.

At the end, we waited for them to come out in their ordinary clothes, and we walked behind them through the streets, very close. Once they stopped, and we banged right into them. I think they did it on purpose, because quite soon after that, Algy suddenly turned round and shouted 'Go home, you horrible little brats!' He started to say a lot more, but Reggie took his arm and tried to make him walk on, but Algy shook him off and really glared at us, with hate, not love.

We went back to Mrs Motherwell's. Dorothy's mother hadn't come back yet.

I don't like to think about it. When Reggie was trying to make Algy walk on, he was saying to him 'Don't be silly, they're only little children!' I don't know if Dorothy heard. I keep remembering.

The new Reference Library will be *round*. I mean, it will *stay* round, not only now when they're building it, and while it's this steel drum-shape. I don't think there's ever been a *round* building before, has there?

Today I was in Oxford Street. I had just come through Piccadilly, past the Henry Watson Music Library, when it was the Two Minutes' Silence. I've never been in Town for the Two Minutes' Silence before.

Everything stopped. I heard the whirring of machines suddenly stopping, and the clicking of typewriters stopping, and shoes scuffling on floors as people stood up. The trams drew up to a halt. And the cart-drivers pulled in their horses, and the horses shook their heads in a great jangling, and then even the jangling stopped. The men took off their hats and stood at attention, and people stood still and alone in the street.

There was total silence and stillness. Then a bird flew across the sky. Only people stop, not birds, because it was only people who did the killing.

Their shouting voices crash through my lilac walls, full of hate. 'She is telling lies!' he is shouting. 'She's M.D., your sister! She's mad! Louis didn't force her! He didn't even touch her!'

What does he mean? Force her to do what?

I am so cold. I stay standing up, till it has been quiet for a long time. Then I sit down on the bed.

Miss Clark said at assembly that someone had reported a girl from our school for sucking a sweet in the street. She had brought disgrace to the school. Outside our formroom Miss Callinan told Miss Tiano it was disgusting, and that streets were for walking in, not for eating and drinking, and the whole country was becoming like a bear-garden. But when I was walking home yesterday there was a whole crowd of men in the street drinking something hot. Nobody's cap came over their ears. Their breath was like dragons'. And I was glad someone was giving them something hot in the street.

On my way home today, I saw some women standing round a huge dustbin. They had wrapped their shawls round their bodies and their heads, and their children were holding on to them and crowding under the shawl too as if they were shy, but I knew they weren't. And a man in a black suit came out of a door and took the lid off the dustbin. I thought at first he was going to find them some rubbish. I thought how horrible, and I was angry and afraid. But he put in a ladle and took out something that clouded into the air. Some of the children shouted out what it was. Soup. And potatoes. And beans. And rice. And peas. And the mothers were wiping their eyes with the end of their shawls.

When I got back home, Jackie Pollack was whizzing downhill on his orange-box sledge. Morrie said that even the big shops in town have sold out of sledges, and everyone in Salford and Manchester is coming to Pollack's because they've got orange-boxes. Even grown-ups have never seen so much snow before.

There were brass bands playing in Oxford Street, marching along with hundreds of people behind, and banners billowing in and out like trombones. I wanted to stand still so that I could watch people's faces; I often do that. But there were so many people on the pavement, not standing still but marching along with them, that I had to walk along too. The music was sad and angry, not pleased with itself and jolly like brass band music generally is. It was crying music.

It is no use talking to Ellie. He says it doesn't mean anything. That grown-ups always quarrel. I wish *I* was far away from them all the time. I wish I didn't hear and see so much.

England Arise

1932

Today is not an ordinary day. I don't just mean it's the first day of the year. I mean today C.P. Scott is dead. He died with the old year. Everyone in the world has been sending messages. Even the King has sent one, saying how sorry he is. The air is trembling, and if you breathe, it trembles inside you. Everyone is whispering. Will everything change? Will the *Manchester Guardian* stop coming? He was Editor for such a long long time, how will they manage without him?

There were thousands of people in Town for the funeral. All the men had their hats off, though they were out in the street, and it was so cold. Their breath was like dragon's breath, and the streets were slushy with grey snow, and grown-ups were crying. I go cold and very tight inside when grown-ups cry.

The *Manchester Guardian* still comes.

I've been looking at the pictures of the funeral. The flowers people have sent, and the people who sent them . . . and the people singing in the Cathedral. I love *Jerusalem*. We sing it on Founders' Day.

> *Give me my bow of burning gold,*
> *Give me my arrows of desire!*

And I love *To be a Pilgrim*. I would have liked to be there too, singing those songs for C.P. Scott at his funeral.

After I'd been looking at the pictures of the funeral yesterday, I turned the page over, and it said that at a Teachers' Conference someone read out a problem from a school arithmetic book. It started 'If three men do in five days the same piece of work that seven women would do in twelve days' . . . and all the teachers laughed. Why did they laugh? Miss Goodwin doesn't laugh when I do them. And if I laughed she'd give me an order mark. I keep thinking about it.

I saw an aeroplane like a magic lantern show in the sky, making a picture on the clouds.

I heard the *New World Symphony* last night. When I came back, they were quarrelling. I could hear them when I went up to bed, but in my head the *New World Symphony* drowned them with echoes and no people and so much empty space.

Today an aeroplane was pulling a streamer behind it. It flew very low as if it was going to hit me, but I didn't move.

> *Terrible as an army with banners.*

I went to *White Horse Inn*! I loved it! I bought the music at Forsythe's, and I'm learning all the songs.

> *Goodbye,*
> *It's time*

I sought a foreign clime
Where I
May find
There'll be hearts more kind
Than I leave behind.

It's so *jaunty*. And funny!

The Opera House, the Palace, the Princes, the Free Trade Hall, the Houldsworth Hall, the Ardwick Empire and Ardwick Green, the Rusholme Theatre . . . So many theatres in Manchester. So many theatres to go to when you just walk everywhere.

People are getting very angry about the aeroplanes. They have written to the *Manchester Guardian*.
Someone says the sky is the only place where the eye can rest . . . But I like it. It's magical.
Anyway, it's playing. I'm glad grown-ups play sometimes.

They are putting slabs of stone over the steel of the Reference Library. It will be snow-white, and round, and enormous, like one of those huge iced wedding-cakes in Meng and Ecker's window in Town.

Twenty down. 'Who has not heard where this you walk?'
'E'er! 'Where'er you walk.'
I do the *Manchester Guardian* crossword every day. I almost always finish it. And I always read *John O'London's Weekly* too – it's full of quotations and people asking if anyone knows the author of something, and it's so exciting, because these are grown-ups I *like*, people who ask these questions and people who know the answers and exchange them, and have fun together.

Kreisler, Szigeti, and Schnabel, all the same week! I can manage one of them. It will be one and threepence. Or is it one and sixpence? Anyway I'll have to choose.

I heard Kreisler playing the Mozart *G Major* at the Free Trade Hall last night. There was no orchestra – just a piano.

And then he played the *Tango*. And in the middle bit of the *Tango*, his violin turns into birds singing, chirruping to each other through the leaves, then swooping down together and up again, in *such joy!* Only Kreisler plays it like that, not Huberman, not Mischa Elman . . . nobody else.

Anyway, a lot of people play so that you know what they're playing is difficult but they can manage it because they're so good. But Kreisler plays it so that it sounds easy, as if anyone can do it.

I could listen to the Albeniz *Tango* for ever. The way the rhythm pushes forward, then pulls back – but only if you play the triplets right. You mustn't make it *pom* pom-pom, like some people do. You have to get the three notes absolutely equal.

I used to think I liked it best played by Sidney on the piano. The sun always seemed to shine through the window right on to the piano keys. Though really the room was dark. All rooms are dark in Salford. Now although I still do love the way he plays it, I'm not quite absolutely sure it's the only right way.

They always make me play at school concerts. The sweat runs down the inside of my legs, and my legs shake. And my hands are so wet, the strings are slippery. And the bow bounces up and down, staggering, because my hands tremble. How do you get people to see you can't bear it? Other people can do it, and people leave them alone. But I can't do it. I can't get people to leave me alone. I don't know how to do it. They say 'You're so calm. You're lucky you're such a calm person.'

★

I'm practising the Beethoven *Rondino*. I don't know why it always comes out *plodding*, instead of skipping.

Huberman, and Lionel Tertis, and Suggia, and Cortot will be playing soon. It's hard to choose. Sometimes I can't go at all, because I've used up all my bus money. I expect I'll go to Huberman.

I want the *Rondino* to sound like a sunny day with clouds blowing, when the air shines like washed windows. But it keeps sounding like the end of a long muddy hike when your heel's blistered and all you want to do is get finished. Why can't I get it to sound right?

In Algebra yesterday Miss Goodwin said 'We'll assume x = 5'. I put up my hand right away, and she said 'Yes, what is it?' and I said 'Why?' She said 'What do you mean?' and I said 'Why should we assume x = 5?' She got annoyed, so I started to explain, but she wouldn't listen.

Why *should* we assume that? Nobody asked if any of us wanted to assume that. If you've got to assume what somebody else says you've got to assume, then perhaps it's just a trick and isn't true.

My mother says she wants me to speak nicely. Not so Lancashire. So I have to take speech lessons from Miss Shaw.

Today Miss Goodwin said again 'We'll assume x = 5'. I put my hand up again. She was just pretending I hadn't said anything about it yesterday. She didn't know whether to notice my hand. She tried not to at first. I said 'Why?' again. I was going to say 'Why can't we assume it's 3?' But she said I was a pest, and trying to be funny. *But I'm trying to understand.* How can we find anything out, if we have Miss Goodwin deciding what we feel like assuming?

It's like Miss Spink's science experiments where if you find out something different from her, she says it's wrong.

I love Algebra. But they never really want you to find anything out. They just want to take charge of everything. But I
want to find things out.

In Salford, whatever street you live in, you can see hills at the end
of it. And you want to be there. It's *part* of being in your street,
being on the hills.

Hardly anyone stays in Salford at the weekend. You get your
rucksack and you take a train – to Hayfield or Edale or anywhere – and start walking. Unless you're in the Clarion
Cycling Club, of course; then you take your bike on the train.
I love those little stations, with buttercups and daisies peeking
through the railings, and one lane running upwards and one
lane running downwards, and the whole world spread out at
the top of a hill.

Cavalcade! The stage *goes round*, with hundreds of people and
scenery on it! *Truly, hundreds* of people! And they step on and off
and it doesn't stop moving! It's amazing!

Something happened in *Cavalcade* that I shall never forget.
There is a scene on a ship, a very happy scene with music and
people dancing. And away from the crowd, two lovers are leaning against the sides of the ship, wanting only to be with each
other, no one else near. The girl is in the man's arms, and they
kiss. And as you watch them, in complete silence a spotlight is
creeping up the dark side of the ship until it rests on its
name . . . H.M.S. TITANIC . . . lingers there . . . and fades
out.

I know about the *Titanic*. Mr Slotki was on the *Titanic*.

Miss Shaw says in words like 'singing' I should make the n and
the g go together. That's called a dipthong. *No. Diphthong.*
(Like Diptheria is *diphtheria*.) She says I say n and g separately,
and I shouldn't. And she says I say y at the end of a word as if

it's double *e*, and it isn't. She gives me exercises to practise, but I don't do them. I'm not interested.

Mad about the boy,
I know it's stupid to be mad about the boy,
I'm so ashamed of it, but must admit
The sleepless nights I've had about the boy

That's Noël Coward. I love it – the rhymes and the tune and the rhythm. Dorothy and I know bits by heart.

Last Sunday I went with Ellie and Benny Rothman and some other people to Hayfield. And at the station, there were hundreds of policemen, and hundreds of people all of them singing!

We started to walk, all of us, hundreds of us, scrambling and climbing. I lost Ellie and Benny right at the beginning, but it didn't matter – two other people had me by the hand. Sometimes I slid down again, but they always caught me and pulled me up again. Everyone was laughing and joking, and singing.

I could still see Benny in and out of the crowd some of the time, but I couldn't see Ellie at all. Once I stopped to get my breath, and I looked back, and Kinder Scout was covered with people like a thick old tree, knobbly and bumpy with lichen.

I never know how to say that word. Lichen.

And then when we were halfway up, a fight started, I don't know how. There were suddenly gamekeepers everywhere, whipping huge sticks through the air, and people grabbing them out of their hands to stop them hitting us. But some people *were* hit, and their faces were bleeding. I didn't know whether to stop where I was, or to go back. But everyone behind me and around me was striding on, and someone had my hand and was pulling me, and I got right up to the top.

And at the top was the wind, the April wind, hurling itself at us at the top of Kinder!

★

In the train back, I had my eyes closed, even though people were singing. I wasn't asleep. Their voices came in and out like a cloud slipping over the moon.

> *England arise,*
> *The long long night is over* . . .

And in the carriage next door, someone started to sing *Kevin Barry*, but stopped, too tired to finish.

> *Just before he faced the hangman,*
> *In his lonely prison cell,*
> *British soldiers tortured Barry*
> *Just because he wouldn't tell*
> *The names of his brave comrades*
> *And other things they wished to know,*
> *'Turn informer, and we'll free you' –*
> *Kevin proudly answered 'No!'*

I don't know what happened to Benny or Ellie. But I saw Ellie next day, so he's not in prison.

Mrs Tiano told me to go with her into the Hall. She said 'Look at those names on the Honours Board.' I looked. She said 'Sylvia Pankhurst . . . Christabel Pankhurst . . . They rebelled about *important* things, not trivial ones like you do. And the school is proud of them.' I nearly burst out laughing. I bet they didn't tell them that at the time. But I kept quiet. Though I was very disgusted.

I've just been thinking that over. I think sometimes grown-ups really *believe* the things they say. *Really* believe they believe . . .

'*Give* me them, *give* me them . . .'

1932–1933

At the Huberman concert I clapped so hard, sitting on the top of the back of the bench, I somersaulted right over it, backwards. And really I half-meant to. Really, I wished the crash had been bigger. I wonder if Huberman saw me, and knew how much I loved his playing, and how excited I felt. If I could have turned cartwheels, I would.

Mrs Gee knows Huberman, and his brother too. She talks to me about them.

The stage doorman at the Opera House says don't I want to see the book. A lot of people have signed since I last looked. Elisabeth Welch, Alice Delysia, Noël Coward, Gertrude Lawrence, Charles B. Cochran, John Gielgud, Gwen Ffrangcon-Davies, Laurence Olivier, George Robey, Billy Danvers, Desiree Ellinger, Enid Stamp-Taylor, Mary Ellis, Robertson Hare, Ralph Lynn, Tom Walls, Winifred Shotter . . . millions more.
    Some of the signatures are bold and black and round. Some are like little scribbling mice. Some are almost like pictures, as if

they've been *drawn* not written. But it's the plays, the shows, that are important, not the signatures. Why do people collect signatures?

The stage doormen get me everyone. They know each other, and pass the book round, between them. They say it's much more sensible than me hanging round the stage doors (I never *do* hang round stage doors. Dorothy does, but not me. And as a matter of fact, it was Dorothy's idea that we should have autograph albums. I never had one when I went to the theatre by myself.) They say they can get them easily for me, when the actors have plenty of time to spare and aren't rushing home.

But I feel bad about having them. There are hundreds, I think. The man at the Opera House said 'One day this will be worth a mint of money,' as if he thought that's why I wanted him to get them. I suppose I can always give it to somebody.

When Dorothy and me are together, suddenly one of us says '*Brrrring brrrring . . . Brrrring brrrring . . . Brrrring brrrring . . . Brrrring brrrring . . .*' until at last the other says sleepily '*Perhaps I'd better answer it after all.*' And then the first one says, sleepily too, '*No, let it ring. I love the tone.*' And we shriek with laughter.

It's Noël Coward. We do it any time at all. In the middle of anything.

'*Old ladies will be trampled to death, struggling to get into the pit. Women will have babies regularly in the upper circle bar during the big scene at the end of the second act . . .*' We do that bit too. Lovely!

I'm playing in Mrs Gee's string quartet. We're playing a *Rasumovsky Quartet*. It's like a ghost story. It makes me shiver.

I'm writing a musical play for school, for everyone to do. Like a Gilbert and Sullivan. I won't write the music – it will take too long for everyone to learn. I'll use music they know already. Bits from *Carmen* and *Rigoletto* and *The Barber of Seville*, that they know the tune of. Then they'll only need to learn the words.

I've just done the Shop scene. It goes to *La Donna Mobile* – not sure how to spell that. It sounds like Moberley, where we sometimes go, but I know the spelling's different.
The customer sings:

> *I want a storybook,*
> *A thrilling and gory book,*
> *Chockful of mystery,*
> *Murders with history.*

Then the shopwalker sings back:

> *Certainly dear Madame –*

and the customer sings:

> *I wondered if you had 'em*

and the shopwalker sings:

> *Madame will soon be served*
> *If Madame will step this way.*

Then a second shopwalker, further down, sings out:

> *Step this way, step this way,*
> *If Madame will step this way.*

and a chorus of all the shop assistants, further and further back, sing out:

> *Step this way, step this way,*
> *If Madame will step this way.*

★

It's fun to do, and easy, and it will be fun and easy to sing too.

I still can't do a tremolo. Mrs Gee shakes my arm just like Mr Cohen used to, but she can't make my hand flop about either. It sticks at the end of my arm as if it's made out of the same piece. She shakes her head. Then she says it will come in time.

She learned violin from Joachim. Joachim was a friend of Brahms. *What I'm saying is*, her teacher was a friend of Brahms! And he was the man who did all the cadenzas – 'Cadenzas by Joachim'!

I once read a poem by Browning, 'And did you once see Shelley plain, and did he stop and speak to you . . .' Sometimes you don't know if something is real, or if it's a bit left over from a dream, still floating in the air.

I like Browning. I like the way he writes a poem as if he's talking. Mozart makes the violin talk too, but in a different way.

That new kind of wire E string cries right through me, tugging at my inside as if my veins are E strings. A chicken would cry like that if it was alive when you plucked it.

> '*Goblin, what are your beads?*'
> '*Green glass, goblin. Why do you stare at them?*'
> '*Give me them, give me them?*'
> '*No.*'

It's a magic poem. Miss Shaw said it at the school concert last night. '*Give* me them, *give* me them'. All the way through, her voice sobbed and cried and moaned like the wind in a drainpipe, or in the telegraph wires; But when she was the nymph it went cold and bright and hard, like the brightness of Estella in *Great Expectations*. I have walked round all day, still hearing it. '*Give* me them, *give* me them.' 'No-o-o-o-o.'

★

I'm going to take all my own books to school and lend them out!
I've worked out how to do it, the cards and the date-stamp –
it will be very easy.

It will be called the Fiction Library. I've got permission!

I'm really excited about the Fiction Library. All my favourite
books – *The Invisible Man*, *The Hound of the Baskervilles*, *Jeremy
and Hamlet*, *Three Men in a Boat*, *The Green Hat*, hundreds of
them – going round and round the school, everyone reading
them and enjoying them!

I love stamping one and giving it to somebody!

Mammy says I'm to coach Sally Sherman for exams.

It's the school dance tonight. I have a turquoise dress that
Mammy made, and silver shoes. All the prefects will be there. I
don't know if I'll dare to dance with them.

Marjorie Pear is so beautiful I could gaze at her all evening.
Like a silver wisp of a moon in a dreaming sky. Or like mother-
of-pearl. Or a rainbow on a petrol puddle. Or the transformation
scene at the theatre when the new scene is just being born.

Her father is Professor Pear at the University. (You say *Peer*,
like looking with your eyes half-closed.) I wonder if *he* is
beautiful too.

And Dagmar Laing. She is very real, not like Marjorie Pear. I
think the word is 'sophisticated'. I am not really sure what that
is, but I think it's the way Dagmar Laing is. Her skin is like
gleaming copper. I think it is that colour from ski-ing. People go
ski-ing in the mountains, in places like Switzerland.

She is wearing a black evening dress, and all her back is bare.
I don't know where to put my hand when I ask her for a dance.
But I don't have her long anyway because it's an excuse-me.

*

141

The other two I specially want to ask are Peggy Neill and Janet Macdonald. They were brilliant in *Much Ado about Nothing*. Neill was Benedict, and Janet was Beatrice. Everyone calls her Neill, not Peggy – Neill with her crisp, fuzzy, semi-shingled hair, and Janet with her long calm plaits that she tosses so neatly over her shoulders.

They were so witty, so loving, so strong. They are the best actors in the school. And still, after the play, they wander about the corridors, hand in hand. And here at the dance I think they'd be quite happy to dance with each other all evening, and not be interrupted by excuse-me's. Everything fizzes all round them, as if they are people in a comic with little lines radiating.

I ask all four of them for autographs. And Janet Macdonald writes:

Be good sweet maid, and let who will be clever . . .

I know lots of people write that in autograph albums, but I keep wondering whether she means something.

Last night was my first night teaching Sally Sherman.

She isn't really interested in books, but that's what the exam is about.

Some of his smart patients came to afternoon tea. They sat on the couch, and I had to hand things round. He put his hand up to my chin, and held it, turning it this way and that, and said to them, 'What do you think of her profile?' I jerked my face away. I almost bit his fingers off.

He talks about how I look, as if I wasn't there, as if I was something he'd bought at Kendal Milne's – that's where he goes to now. I said 'I'm not one of your smart women patients!' and walked out of the room.

★

I went to the pictures yesterday and saw *Svengali*. The book is called *Trilby* – I've read it. The girl who's Trilby looks like Yiven – Yiven who went to Derby Street. Her name is Marion Marsh, and John Barrymore is Svengali.

Svengali makes Trilby sing. It's her voice that sings, but Svengali makes it happen, and he owns it, he owns her. Like my father thinks he owns everyone.

The best thing to do – the *only* thing really – is to stop trying to teach Sally about English literature because she just doesn't understand or want to know, and instead teach her how to pass exams. That's stupid really, but it's simpler, and it keeps grown-ups happy.

I've seen *Richard of Bordeaux*. I can't stop thinking about it. Gwen Francon Davies is plain really, but so very lovely. How can that be? It's because she and Richard are so much in love. It's the way he touches her, the way the back of her neck curves – what do you call that? . . . The nape . . . the way he kneels and puts his head in her lap . . . I want to cry. I want to *shout*. She's *radiant* – that's the right word, not beautiful. Gwen Ffrangcon-Davies. I must spell it right. John Gielgud is so gentle, and they don't value him. They think men should hurt and kill.

'. . . How Robert would have laughed . . .' I keep hearing Richard say it and my throat hurts as if I'd never had my tonsils out.

He's having his nails manicured now. At Lewis's. Manicured!

I've discovered something magic. If I'm walking out in the street, and a man is coming towards me, a young man, and I stare right into his eyes, he *has* to look back. He can't *not* do it. He's surprised, but he *has* to do it. It's so exciting. I want to sing and shout and laugh. It's funny!

I hope Sally gets through. I'm doing the best I can, writing things down for her and telling her to learn them off by heart.

I can't bear *King Lear*, and *The Taming of the Shrew*, and *Hansel and Gretel*. I don't want to see them lying about anywhere, or hear people talking about them!

I'm invited to a party at Sally Sherman's. I really don't want to go, but I have to. This will be the second party I've ever been to.

He really does love his nails. I think a *girl* does it for him!

I went to Sally Sherman's party. It was nothing but telephone calls – people telephoning her to say they couldn't come, or were coming later, or they were *answering* the telephone, or they were talking about people who had telephoned them yesterday or the day before or the day before that. And everyone was a 'boy-friend'. I hate that word. Either someone's a friend or a lover.

They laughed when I went to the piano, but when I began to play, Oh the excitement on their faces! I played the first few bars of Beethoven's immortal *Moonlight Sonata*, and as the notes died away . . . 'Where did you get that lovely *singing* tone?' they exclaimed . . . That isn't quite right. I must learn it properly, and say it very dramatically, without laughing. It's always in the *Humourist*. A big advertisement, with a drawing.

I was looking at that book again in my father's bookcase, the one I used to look at years ago, and I've suddenly seen that it isn't a cockatoo at all – it's a penis. In 'an advanced stage of syphilis', it says. How funny. All those years I puzzled over it. It does look rather like a cockatoo . . . but not quite . . .

I have a rash. It started weeks ago, but it's so bad now I can't go to school. I can't go anywhere. My face is so burning that you can hold your hand inches away from it, and feel it flaming.

The skin specialist said there's nothing he can do. He says even a drop of water makes it flare up. The skin is hysterical, he says. He sounds angry about it, as if I'm doing it on purpose.

I have to wash my face with a bag of oatmeal. I have to wet the bag and dab it on my face. It smells horrible. When it's dry I have to dab calomine on it, very thick and white, to try to cool it.

They sent me home. Because when I met Miss Goodwin in the corridor, she smiled, and said 'Good morning', and I started to cry. I don't mean with a sound. Tears just ran down my face for no reason and I couldn't stop them. I wish people wouldn't speak to me. It always makes me cry. I'm all right if people leave me alone.

I keep being sent home from school. They say they can't teach me if I cry when anyone speaks to me.
    It doesn't matter anyway. I've passed all my exams, and got good marks.

They want me to go to Oxford or Cambridge, but I won't go. They do you such a favour, these colleges. You have to be so grateful because there are some special colleges they're *allowing* girls to go to. I don't want special favours. Boys can go to any place they want to, even if they haven't got the marks I have. I'm just going to be a writer.

'J'

1933–1934

Dorothy says she's going to have a German pen friend. I didn't know she could. I know Queenie's got one, but she takes German.

Miss Tiano said everyone can have one, even if you don't take German, because there are lots of them asking.

Dorothy has written to her German girl and said 'I'm Jewish. I don't suppose you'll want to write to me.'

She's had a letter back. It says 'I like Jews.'

Dorothy's written again, but her father has found out and won't let her send it. She's very upset and surprised. She says her father has never stopped her doing anything before.

Her father says it's very dangerous.

★

Dorothy says she doesn't care, she's not frightened.

Dorothy's father says, 'Not dangerous for *you*. Dangerous for *the girl*.'

He said the German girl would be in great trouble – her whole family would be in great trouble – if anyone found out she was writing to Dorothy.

Dorothy hasn't answered her letter. I'm sorry the girl will never know why. I think people should always know why.

I spent almost the whole day at the Ref. Today was the first day you can go in. There are thousands of books, and you can take any one you want off the shelf and take it to a table and read it. There are hundreds of people reading. But you have to be very careful when you push your chair back because it echoes and echoes right round the room, and you feel like someone in a Bateman cartoon in the *Humourist*, all the elderly men staring at you in horror, and you get smaller and smaller like a lump of snow melting away.

The new Ref is a wonderful place. The King is going to open it, but not till the summer.

Miss Shaw is a member of the Unnamed Society. They're called that because none of them has their name on the poster.

The Unnamed Society is doing *Murder in the Cathedral*, I think at the Palace, but I'm not sure, and six of us in our form are going to be in the Chorus with the real actors, and I'm one of them! We all stand together (I could never stand there by myself) and chant every now and then. I'm not mad keen on the play, but it has some good sounds in it. 'Living, and partly living . . .' Isn't that bleak? I know what it means.

The others are going with Miss Weiss to visit prisons! It makes me so angry. They all have this Grand Pash on her, and they're being very good and angel-like together.

They have philosophical discussions about prisons, all trying to be more compassionate than anyone else, so that Miss Weiss will answer them in her serious well-educated Oxford voice, and they'll swoon.

They rub themselves against the idea of Strangeways like a cat rubbing itself against your leg. They make me sick. If I ever went to Strangeways, I would go on my own, and probably because I was visiting a friend. Not because I was in the Junior Sixth, with a pash on Miss Weiss.

I keep reading in the *Manchester Guardian* the terrible things that are happening to Jewish people in Germany. If they are old, and can't get up when they are knocked down . . . It makes me feel ill, but I have to read it. I have to know.

A bill came this morning. Daddy said 'A wine bill! For Ellie!' At first he couldn't speak any more – he really wanted to get the strap. Then he said 'I'll give him wine bills! The young teival!' (that means 'devil') and he was *pleased*.
   He was angry but he was *pleased*. He said he would borrow the money from someone to pay for it. I could see he was going to boast about it. And he said again, *admiringly*, 'I'll give him wine bills, the young teival.' Mammy was not pleased. She looked as if she thought it was wicked.

I've been spending days in the Ref, reading Susan Isaac's two fat books, *Intellectual Growth in Young Children*, and the other one about Social Development. I like the first one best. She tells you the things the children did or said, and gives their ages. That wonderful bit about Tommy, when the children had been carrying cans of water into the garden to paint, and she said they'd better not do it any more because they'd got their feet wet. And

Tommy took all the flowers out of every vase on every table, and poured the water into his can, and then he put all the flowers back into every vase and every vase back on its table, and he walked out into the garden, *beaming* – (I can see that!) – saying 'Tommy's got water now!'

They weren't glass vases. They were pottery! He couldn't see the water but he knew it was inside! He remembered!

He was 2:8 – that's two years and eight months.

I shall always remember him.

I love this book.

Whenever I open a book, a capital J leaps out at me.

Mosley's fascists have opened a headquarters at the bottom of our street. But nobody says anything. As if it isn't happening.

Is there a J on that page? Or have I imagined it? I have to look.

The *Jewish Chronicle* says we must always behave well. Not make a fuss, or draw attention to ourselves, or ask for special treatment.

Ellie went to London for the Mosley meeting, and he's come back looking as if he was chased all the way from London to Manchester by ghosts and only just slammed the front door in time. It is really scary.

He says the whole of the back of the platform was covered by an enormous Union Jack. There was a huge spotlight on Mosley. And if anyone in the audience said a word, a spotlight immediately lit them up and about a dozen Blackshirts hurled themselves at them from all sides of the hall and dragged them outside, and then about a dozen more Blackshirts started kicking them and beating them as they lay on the pavement. And the police were arresting the people who were being beaten!

I've only just realised that 'natives' means whoever's born in that country! And all these years I thought it meant black people, or savages, or people who danced round a missionary in a stew-pot! But *I'm* a native! Everyone is, when they're in their own country! Why do people tell you lies?

It's like a torch in the darkness, dripping fire. A capital J. I'm frightened. There's always one on the page, leaping out.

These smart women who come to tea, with their coloured nail polish and lipstick, and who hang on his words as if he's God, while my mother (no coloured nail polish, no lipstick) pours out tea for them from our silver teapot that lives in the cabinet with the willow-pattern plates . . . and I have to hand round scones . . . He tells them – no, he *declaims* – about the latest book he's read, or the latest play he's read! And I've already read exactly the same words in the *Manchester Guardian*! And I *know* he hasn't read the book! And I *know* he hasn't seen the play! And I get furious, because I'm so ashamed, and I shout 'You *haven't* seen that play! Why do you say you have! Why do you tell such lies!' And I walk out of the room, trembling.

There are two very beautiful sisters – people call them the Preger twins – who my father is very keen on. I can't tell them apart. They really are very lovely . . . like the new moon when it is just a curl of silver hair. I saw one of them in the waiting room this afternoon. I was coming down the stairs. The waiting room's our hall really, so you have to come down into it, and I hate it because everyone in the waiting room stares as you come down. But I saw her, and I just stopped for a moment on the stair and caught my breath, because she was so beautiful.

My father is starting to call all these people by their first name. I don't know if he does it when he's talking to them when they're in his surgery, but he does it when he's talking *about* them. 'Tolza', he says, or used to say. Today he called her 'Tot'. She's one of the Preger sisters. I don't know which one. Anyway, they have different names now, because they are married.

One of the people I have to deliver medicine to is 'Tot'. Those bottles and pill-boxes beautifully wrapped in brilliant white paper, with a splash of scarlet sealing-wax . . . I walk through Broughton Park, the houses with names, the mountain-ash berries hanging from the fringed trees like sealing wax, and I knock at the door.

I used to hate it when I knocked and I knew the door would open, and I would have to speak. Now I don't mind. The door opens. I just say 'For Mrs Freeman.' I hand it in, and go away again.

I'm always delivering medicines to Mrs Freeman. Beautiful snowy-white packages, pleated like little ball-gowns, fastened with scarlet buttons.

Yesterday, after I'd handed the packet in, I saw in the garden a pram with a baby sitting in it, a dumpy baby with a bonnet on, not a bit like silvery 'Tot', who stares at me. Her lip wobbles, her eyes accuse me of coming into her garden, and I think her face is likely to splinter across any moment. I stop, and talk softly to her, and take my florin out of my pocket and show it to her.

I tip it in the sun so that it flashes, the baby is curious and holds out her hand for it. I put it in her palm, and she raises it to her mouth, licks it very delicately and carefully (seeming to *listen* to the taste), looks at it again. I put my hand out to take it back, but she won't give it me! I don't know how to get it back! It's my concert money! How do you get something back from a baby? What shall I do?

In the end I leave it with her.

This afternoon my father spoke to me.
Red Letter Day.
Neither of us could handle it.
He couldn't bear to find himself talking to me, and actually

trying to say something that he thought was friendly. And me –
after all these years – my heart stopped, and then began to beat
very carefully.

He tried to smile. He said 'It was very nice of you to give
Mrs Freeman's baby your money yesterday.' And he held out a
florin.

I was furious. I said 'It was nothing to do with you! It was
between me and the baby! It was private!' And I wouldn't take it.
Not even though it had been my concert money!

He won't even let you own your relationships. Everything has
to be his.

Sometimes I watch the Theatre of Action performing in the
street. I always get the feeling they're performing on the top of
telegraph poles. I mean, when I look back, that's what I see them
doing.

I think it's because they act in such a non-human way, like
insects, with very dead props like square boxes and bits of metal.

If I had something to say, I'd want to say it so that people
would listen. But everyone hurries by, coat collar turned up, as
if the Theatre of Action was bad weather.

At this moment one man, and one dog who has nothing to
do with him but has just wandered up and is peeing against a
Snofrute carton, turning it yellow, is the only audience. And me,
of course.

Actually I do like that Ernst Toller thing they do. 'They honour
the dead who serve the living.' I mean, I like that line, not the
way they do it.

There's a bit in Gluck's *Orpheus – Dance of the Blessed Spirits*, I
think – that, if you played it more slowly, could be a funeral
march . . . a funeral song . . . I've begun to write words to it . . .

> *We are your mourners, your blood burns in our blood,*
> *Your courage our heritage fires a new love.*

Your life in our life, this be your epitaph,
'Honour the dead and the living serve'.

I know this doesn't say exactly the same thing. Just losing 'They'
alters the sense.

It isn't terribly good yet. I'll make it better. But actually, political poems never are terribly good. It's as if someone outside is
telling you what to write, even though you believe it's you that's
writing.

All the same, I find myself singing that song I've written. I suppose it's just that the music is haunting, and the words aren't
fighting it, or competing with it, but just go along with it . . . A
funeral song for Ernst Toller . . . 'We are your mourners, your
blood burns in our blood . . .'

I am writing all the time. Prose, and poetry.

The school magazine will be out soon. I can't think of anything
else.

I've gone in for practically every literary competition in the
magazine. I always do. Every time it comes out, I'm frightened
to get my copy to see what I've got printed. And I'm so happy
when I see it.

I met Miss Fletcher on the stairs this morning. She stopped and
said 'Congratulations'. I said 'What do you mean?' I was frightened to know. She said 'Don't you know? You've got all the
prizes. Not much for anyone else, is there?' I thought she was
making a friendly joke. I had wanted to smile at the wonderful
news. I had started to smile, I think. But there was an odd tone
to her voice. Did she mean it was wicked of me? Was I destruc-
tive to write for the magazine? I gave up the smile halfway.

I got my report this afternoon. In the General Remarks bit, Miss

Hawcidge has written 'Leila has given most efficient voluntary help in the Fiction Library'. How funny. Wasn't it *my* library that I gave? There *wasn't* the Fiction Library before . . . I sometimes don't know what happens and what doesn't happen . . . what's true and what isn't true.

Out of Bounds

1935

The Cohens' house is the noisiest and messiest I've ever been in. The wireless is on all the time, but everyone is moving round. I mean, no one is sitting and listening to it. And people are walking about eating or drinking – slab of bread in one hand, cup of tea in the other – and arguing. I don't think they ever sit down to have a meal. In fact, now that I think of it, they hardly ever sit down at all. It's like people say you've got splinters in your bum.

They do have a couch, but they throw clothes on it – coats, jerseys, gloves, socks, especially very long thick knitted scarves. If you burrowed a foot or so deep, you might possibly find a visitor left behind from nights back, someone who didn't know no one sat down in the Cohens' house.

I've joined The Youth Front against War and Fascism, and they're in it.

I don't mean Raymond and Cecil Cohen. This is a different lot.

We were coming over St James's croft, all the six Cohens, and

Annie and me, everyone of course arguing, and Ike suddenly thumped me on the back and burst out laughing. He's enormous, Ike is. (The other Cohens, some are plump and some are slight, but they're all much smaller than Ike. You'd never know any of them are related to each other at all.) And when he thumped me like that, I nearly swallowed my teeth, even though they aren't false, and I couldn't speak for several minutes. He was shouting in that roaring way he has. 'Did you hear her? She said *bleddy*! Did you hear? She said *bleddy!*' I read somewhere 'mortified'. That's what I was (how do you know things like that? With words? How can you tell what mortified means?) I said 'I didn't. I said bloody.' He said, not taking any notice, and dancing about on the croft like a circus elephant, 'She said bleddy. She said bleddy!' Everyone was laughing.

Ike is so huge! A roaring prophet with a Burnley accent. He roars 'Gerraway!' and nudges you with his elbow in a confiding way, and you fly into space.

Judy is the intellectual of the family. They all talk about Marx and Engels and Keir Hardie and the Chartists, but Judy's the one who always knows the page and the paragraph and the absolutely exact quotation. (Well, I don't know myself, so maybe it isn't exact, but it sounds good.)

He's called Judy – sometimes Jude – but his name is really Julius. (Funny really. One of the girls is Toby. But no Punch.) Actually Toby is a Yiddish word; or is it Hebrew? – it means dove, not Dog Toby at all. But she's much more like a dog, a nice solid bouncy dog, than a dove.

Judy's a chemist. All the boys go to work. I don't know what school the girls go to.

They're always saying 'Straight up – no messing!'

Except Judy. He only says intellectual things.

★

Annie says they sing *Kevin Barry* at their school. I mean, they all stand up and sing it, at prayers – teachers as well! She goes to a Catholic school so I expect they're nuns, the teachers. Fancy having nuns teaching you! English people aren't supposed to sing *Kevin Barry*. But we do. We sing it loudly together, walking over the croft.

> *'Shoot me like an Irish soldier,*
> *Do not hang me like a dog,*
> *For I fought to free old Ireland*
> *On that still September morn,*
> *All around that little bakery,*
> *Where we fought them hand to hand,*
> *Shoot me like an Irish soldier,*
> *For I fought to free Ireland.'*

I like *The Love Song of J. Alfred Prufrock* best of anything of T.S. Eliot's. 'I should have been a pair of ragged claws, Scuttling across the floors of silent seas . . .' I know how that feels. I know it often.

And 'That is not what I meant at all. That is not it, at all.' When my mother had said she wished I would talk to her more and not be so secretive, and one day I did, that day in Leicester Road, and she looked at me as if she was wondering who I was . . . bewildered. 'That is not what I meant at all.'

I'm sorry he's gone all churchy now. Before, he was talking to everyone. Poetry isn't meant to divide people up, like picking a team.

Annie, Leah and Toby are going to work in the mill together. Toby wasn't going to, at first. She thought she might be a chemist, like Judy. But now she is.

I just can't believe it. It's too horrible! Christians say you have to beat babies! I mean really babies! Before they're a year old! And I mean really *beat* them, with sticks and belts! Till they don't have any will of their own, it says! Because if they have any will of their own, they'll go to Hell! It's in a book Annie's got, a Christian religious book. She showed it to Toby and me. It made me feel really sick.

I think grown-ups are mad. Not only cruel, but mad. I wish children didn't have to be born from grown-ups! And they're in charge! They're in charge of the world!

We marched over St James's Croft, all the Cohens and Annie and me, singing *England arise, the long long night is over* as loudly as we could. The gypsies had gone, and there was no one else there.

> *People of England, all your valleys call you,*
> *High in the rising sun the lark sings clear . . .*
> *Shall it die unheard,*
> *That sweet pleading word —*

Not '*pleading*'! Not 'sweet *pleading*'! That's horrible. How can William Morris say 'pleading'? When I'm so enraged!

But the last verse is like trumpets ringing out —

> *Forth then, ye heroes, patriots and lovers,*
> *Comrades of danger, poverty and scorn,*
> *Mighty in faith of Freedom your great mother,*
> *Giants refreshed in Joy's new rising morn.*
> *Come and swell the song,*
> *Silent now so long,*
> *England is risen! And the day is here!*

We sing out so loudly as we tramp along, arms round each other, that two little children in ragged white shifts with nothing underneath come up to us and stand staring. And we catch our breath, and smile at them. Oh, that was good! Like 'Bring me my bow of burning gold!'

We all went to the pictures Saturday night — Judy, Ike, Toby and

the rest. There was a Pathé news reel on – about *Lord* Derby!
Lord Derby! The *Earl of Derby!* They pronounced it *Darby*, not
Derby, and he *let* them! He never stopped them, just smiled at
them like a fool, as if *they* knew how to pronounce it better than
he does. Sucking up to them. And at the very end he saw them
out, and he shook hands with them, and he said 'I 'ope you 'ave
a good 'unt' – in broad Lancashire! He must have been practising the sentence for days! And we all banged our seats and fell
about. Ike sounded like an elephant crashing through the jungle,
trumpeting. We still keep saying it to each other – shaking hands,
and saying 'I 'ope you 'ave a good 'unt,' and collapsing.

We have been out canvassing for Frank Allaun. Judy, Toby, and
all of us. Why 'canvassing'? Strange word.

No one has written for a violin E string like Mozart. I sit on the
floor listening, and I close my eyes and shake my head, and the
tears clot my lashes. He *talks*. He makes the violin *talk*. He
clutches you, whispers and pleads and *begs* you.

A chap at the Cohens' last night – a big chap, much older than
me – he said to me 'Your Dad used to teach me at Derby Street.
He was a bastard. They were all real ripe bastards – *beaters* – but
he was the worst.'

Ellie has come in. I sit there again in the dark, waiting for the
song to come through the chink of light round the edge of the
downstairs door.

> *You are my heart's delight,*
> *And where you are,*
> *I long to be . . .*

It slips slowly down my face, hanging on, like tears.

Ellie has invited me up to Cambridge for May Week. He says that's something special. I think he wants to show me off to his friends.

Nearly every night now, at eleven or twelve o'clock, Ellie comes home and switches on the wireless. And when I hear the orchestra starting up, I slip out of bed, and settle on the top stair. And when Tauber sings *Shine* . . . 'Shine, then, my whole life through' . . . the top note rings out like shivering cymbals, and I close my eyes and shake my head, because I almost can't bear it.

I can't get it out of my head. I think, sometimes, one song, one book, one symphony, would last me for ever, just one of each, over and over.

Here, in Cambridge, they talk about T.S. Eliot, and Louis MacNeice, and Auden and Spender and Day Lewis. And Marx and Engels.

People here are so *excited* about poetry . . . the way they wait for books to come out, and rush to the bookshop to buy them . . . something happening, like going to the theatre!

> *Dan Dan Dan,*
> *The Communist Party man,*
> *Working underground all day,*
> *Sending fraternal greetings*
> *To secretariat meetings,*
> *Never sees the light of day,*
> *TA RA RA*
> *Dan Dan Dan . . .*

It goes on for ever.

One of them took me on the river in a boat . . . a punt, was it? I've read about that, and how you trail your fingers in the water, and drift under weeping willows, so I wanted that to happen. I sort of willed it to happen, and it did. It was interesting . . .

Another one tried to flirt with me. That always irritates me.

Why don't people say straight out what they want, or else say nothing.

One is very tall and fair and good-looking, with curly hair. Another one is smallish and dark and rather ugly and sinister. They all seem to be called either John or James; except the girl – she's Margot. She's one of the Johns' girls, or one of the James's. Her hair is dark, and her breasts are large and heavy and flat on top like a doorstep. Not two separate parts. She's kind to me, in a looking-after big-sister sort of way, as if she feels responsible because I'm young. Not fiddling about with me and wondering if she can experiment with me, like the men.

John Cornford's mother is Frances Cornford – 'Oh fat white woman whom nobody loves . . .'

> *My very intelligent sister,*
> *In Moscow is doing her best,*
> *The Commissars cannot resist her,*
> *And you can imagine the rest.*
> *My God, my God, my God how the money rolls in, rolls in,*
> *My God, my God, my God how the money rolls in.*

They're always singing it. They're good for songs.

Whenever anyone stands up and speaks, he stretches out his arm, bends it at the elbow, holds out something invisible to you on the palm of his hand, his fingers curved round it so that it won't fall off, and shakes it up and down. 'Comrades! At this moment in time!' 'Comrades, it is no accident . . .!'

Even if they were saying 'John, you know I don't like crumpets!' they would do it.

Ellie does it all the time. Even Margot does it. They laugh among themselves, and call it The Cambridge Clutching Hand.

But they wouldn't want me to laugh at it. It's something very powerful, like a secret sign.

★

161

They have servants to polish their shoes, and take their trousers to be pressed, and clean their room, and bring them tea and toast! (Ellie too!) They talk a lot but what else do they do?

I hardly say a word – though I love the songs.

I am a Trade Union leader,
I follow Citrine and Bevin,
The rank-and-file call me a bleeder,
But God, how the money rolls in!
My God, my God, my God how the money rolls in, rolls in,
My God, my God, my God how the money rolls in.

I sing 'Gawd' in that line. 'But *Gawd!* how the money rolls in.'

And the other thing is, this magazine that Ellie and his Cambridge friends have got, I really enjoy it. It makes me laugh with excitement. *Out of Bounds*, it's called. It's got out by the Romilly twins, Giles and Esmond. Ellie says they're Winston Churchill's nephews. It's full of protests – marches with banners – like demanding the right to masturbate, or the right not to be beaten.

Really it's for public school boys. But our school is a sort of public school. I'll volunteer to sell it.

With Grass in her Hair

1935–1936

I've taken half a dozen *Out of Bounds* to sell. I'll get Margaret, Queenie, and Dorothy to buy one – that makes four, with me. I'd only have to find two more. The trouble is, I don't think people in my form even know what masturbation means.

Not just what it *means*. What it *is*.

I don't really understand. Doesn't everybody masturbate?

The first time I saw that copy of *Out of Bounds*, that was full of pictures of banners demanding the Right to Masturbate, I thought it was a joke. In fact, I thought I hadn't seen anything so funny for a long time. Because I couldn't see how anyone *didn't* have the Right to Masturbate – how anyone could take it away from them. But I've just realised that if you sleep in a dormitory, like public school boys do, you can never do private things. I think that's very sad. It must be terrible.

At public schools, some boys are given the *privilege* of beating other boys. *The privilege!* Adults are so hateful I don't want to have anything to do with them. I wish children could be born out of children.

*

163

I don't think anyone in our form is old enough to read *Out of Bounds*. I'm really *bullying* people to buy it. I mean, *arguing* with them. I argued with Queenie yesterday. And Dorothy. I mean, I tried to *make* them buy it. I mean, I tried to make them *want* to buy it – which is ridiculous.

I'm spending every minute now translating Greek poetry and Latin poetry into English verse.

> *Let's live and love, my Lesbia, and despise*
> *The harsh disgruntled talk of stern old men.*
> *The sun may set each night and rise again,*
> *But for us mortals, when the light once dies,*
> *Remains for ever but the void of night*
> *And one long sleep.*
> > *Oh Lesbia, let us kiss!*
> *Kiss me a thousand times! Each one is bliss!*
> *And then a thousand more . . .*

It went very easily, almost of its own accord. So I don't know why so much time has gone.

This is a really lovely book, *Wright's Book of Latin Prose and Verse*. You have to translate *freely*, or it would thump about like a sack of potatoes; but it still has to be the poem you started with. It's fascinating. Fascinate . . . Fascinare . . . it means to enchant. Catullus likes that word.

I've had *Sons and Lovers* out of the school library three times this term. It's in the locked cupboard, so you have to ask for the key, and sign for it.

I think I'm the only person in the place signing in that large black library book for books from the locked cupboard.

Strange what fun sonnets are to write. I mean generally I hate having to follow rules. But with some things it's really stimulating. A bit like the *Manchester Guardian* crossword puzzle. Or like tying up Houdini.

Last week Ellie took me to Simon and Ivy's, in Devonshire Street. They're in the Youth Front but actually they're grown-up and even have a little girl. Their house doesn't have much in it, so we all lay on the floor and talked and sang, and one person even slept.

> *Alleluia I'm a bum,*
> *Alleluia bum again,*
> *Alleluia give us a handout*
> *To revive us again.*

It's good to have somewhere to go.

Everyone goes to Simon and Ivy's. The Cohens, Annie, Nat Lerner. Nat Frayman sometimes . . . No one asks questions. They just give you a mug of tea and let you be. I like being in their family, I think they're Catholic.

I've had my latch key taken away again.

It doesn't matter. Elia's got one. He's at home now, on vacation. (That's holiday. Like he's called Elia now.)

He goes dancing, with Ray Garber I suppose (does she call him Elia now?), so I wait in the backyard for him to come back, and he lets me in. He's always back later than me. Lucky, or I'd have to climb in through a window – which I've actually got very good at, even though I didn't take gym.

It's very cold, waiting in the little shed out in the yard. The evening is damp and blue, and the street lamps have haloes round them. I stamp my feet – but not too loudly in case someone hears. Last night I had to wait a long time, but I knew he was out, and he did turn up in the end.

*

165

I hope I get my key back before he starts again.

There is a big picture of Mrs Freeman on the wall. Not a photograph – a painting. Just her face and her shoulders.

Somehow it makes me think of the picture of *The Last Watch of Hero*, and *Hope*, and *Captive Andromache*, and *Ophelia* – or is it *The Lady of Shalott* – floating down the river, all of those pictures of my father's.

Who has painted it? Why is it there? It is very lovely, silvery and misty like the moon.

My mother wants me to teach at Uncle Larry's Bible classes. I suppose she thinks it would be good for my character. At first I said I wouldn't. Then I said if Uncle Larry would come with me to the Theatre of Action's production of *Till the Day I Die*, then I'd teach at his Bible classes.

He's actually coming. I didn't think he would!

I'm still trembling from *Till the Day I Die*. That scene when the Nazi says 'I suppose you know Beethoven's *Violin Concerto*? . . . in the key of D? . . . with the Joachim cadenzas?' And then smashes his rifle-butt on to his hands, breaking his fingers so he can't play any more. I felt sick.

When we came out Uncle Larry said 'Why do you want to see such unhappy things? A girl like you . . .' I was so full of rage and pity that I couldn't speak.

Elia is back from London. He went to see a play called *England Expects* – a very funny play. Well, it's meant to be very noble and patriotic, but the audience has learned all the words, and chants them all the way through with the actors, while the author sits in a box, looking very bewildered, Elia says.

It's packed out every night. It's like being in a club.

★

We all went to the Yorkshire moors last week-end and had a camp – a huge Socialist Camp – the Youth Front, the Ramblers, and Clarion Cycling Club, and the Woodcraft Folk, and the Co-op Women's Guild (Annie's in both of those, which makes us all laugh. She's not a *woman!*) and the Y.C.L. (that's Young Communist League) and the Labour League of Youth. And the Challenge Film Club.

Some boy I'd never seen before asked me to come for a walk with him in the dark, and when we'd been out for a while he said we were lost and he didn't know where we were. I hate it when someone gets into a panic, specially if it's a boy. I stopped speaking to him, and in the end I found the way back, and he followed me, and I went into the girls' tent without saying a word to him.

The camp-fire is burning. We are all rolled in blankets, sometimes two people together. And someone called Paddy is singing a song.

> *I am the man, the very fat man,*
> *Who waters the workers' beer.*
> *I am the man the very fat man,*
> *Who waters the workers' beer.*
> *And what do I care if it makes him ill,*
> *If it makes him terribly queer?*
> *I've a car and a yacht and an aeroplane,*
> *And I waters the workers' beer.*

He's Irish, and he sings it in a lilting gentle Irish voice, like my Uncle Larry who only sings songs like *The Mountains of Mourne*, and Hebrew prayers, not *The Very Fat Man*.

I love it!

And then we sing *England Arise* –

> *Forth then ye heroes, patriots and lovers,*
> *Comrades of danger, poverty and scorn . . . !*

*

And then the *Internationale.*

I am so sleepy from the smoke. Someone will pull me out of my sleeping-bag in the morning, to help collect eggs from the farmer.

I must remember the tent must be absolutely dry, before we re-pack it. Otherwise it goes mouldy.

There was a boy called Fred at the camp. He kept staring at me. I stared at the sky.

I've written a play for Uncle Larry's classes. It's about Moses and the crossing of the Red Sea. Moses is a sort of Y.C.L.'er, working with this huge crowd of people, some of them friends, some of them enemies, some weak, some jealous, some agent-provocateurs . . . I'm enjoying it; and the kids are enjoying it too. It's very good having a company to practise with.

I'm in a very little place called Chamonix! It's abroad! On the Continent! And it's *ski-ing!* I've gone with Elia and his Cambridge friends, and a *lecturer.* A big man, like a shaggy bear. They call him Haldane.

I am learning to ski. I come rushing down the slope, shouting 'Attention! Attention!' (that's French), and always fall over. I enjoy it. Everyone laughs.

Today I got lost. The snow was so very deep, I had to raise my knee almost up to my forehead every time I dragged my foot out. It's very tiring doing that. I got slower and slower, and it got darker and darker, and everyone got further and further ahead of me until they were out of sight. I just kept going on.

I was still going on when a sledge came back for me. And a man got out, lifted me in, and covered me with a very smelly rug. I don't know what was pulling the sledge. Maybe a goat. It was pitch dark.

When we got to the hut, there was a big fire blazing. No one took much notice of me coming in.

I found two bites on my wrist and began to scratch them. Someone came near me and said – it was Haldane – 'Those are flea-bites. You can always tell flea-bites, because they're very close together like those are. You'll have to go to your room, and spread out a big white sheet, and stand in the middle of it, and take off your clothes one by one, and give it a good shake each time, and you can see the flea when it falls on the sheet, and you have to squash it.

'But it's better of course if someone else is there to do that. I'll come with you.'

I wasn't sure if he meant it. I looked at him. He looked quite serious. But I laughed and stayed by the fire.

Haldane tells me today that what you should do if ever you're afraid, is to go on doing the thing that frightens you until you've exhausted the reaction. That's what he says, 'exhausted the reaction'.

Today we were on our way back to catch the boat train. They always go so fast, and I can't keep up with them.

I still can't understand what the row was about, or why I almost got arrested. I was just walking along, trying to find the others, and quite a crowd collected around me. They got more and more angry, and started shouting at me – very fast, so that I couldn't understand a word – and clenching their fists, and waving their arms. And eventually someone went and got a gendarme, and he started shouting at me too. I thought I was going to end up in prison or something. I kept saying 'Je ne comprends pas. Je suis anglaise.' I thought if I kept on saying nothing but that, they would have to let me go.

Why are Paris people so angry?

Anyway, in the end he didn't arrest me, and everyone went

away, grumbling, and I managed to get to the train. I don't think anyone had even noticed I was missing.

But I still don't know why they were so angry. I think perhaps they didn't like me wandering round Paris in ski-ing clothes. And not being French. And being a girl. I think, maybe, they have rules about how you have to be.

The Challenge Film Club is in Cheetham Hill. We sit on wooden benches and watch Eisenstein or Pudovkin or Dovchenko. Nobody has seen those Russian films but us, me and the Cohens and Annie and Lou and Nat and other Challenge people, because Salford Council's banned them. But luckily the Challenge Club's in Manchester.

I think about them in bed. The woman's smashed glasses as she lies on the flight of steps . . . And that little boy, seen through the legs of the huge horses, as if he was standing in a doorway . . . Pictures stay in your mind.

When I came back from Simon and Ivy's, I put my key in the lock, but the door wouldn't open. They'd bolted me out.

I took my key out of the lock very carefully, without making a sound. I could hear someone breathing on the other side of the door. Waiting for me to beg.

I tiptoed down the steps and halfway down the street. Then I began to walk very fast back to Simie and Ivy's.

They were very surprised to see me again. I told them I was locked out. Simon said 'Are you sure?' He said 'Did you ring?' I nodded. I said 'Can I sleep here?' He rumpled his hair. He said 'Well, of course you can if you have to. But I'll come back with you first and make sure they really won't let you in.' I was angry. They'd never asked me questions before, and I didn't like him coming back with me to make sure. But I had to let him. We walked along, not talking, and when we got to our house, I put my key in the door again, very very quietly, and turned it and pushed, very gently. I could still hear someone breathing on the other side, and I didn't want them to know I was there. Then Simie said 'Ring'. So I pressed the bell, just a little, on one side, so that it wouldn't make any sound. I kept my finger there a long time. After a bit Simie said, in a rather tired voice, 'All right. Come on then.' And we went back to his house.

I have come home. The door was unbolted again. I walked in. My father and mother were quarrelling. They stopped when they saw me. I walked past them – between them, actually. They moved apart when they saw me – and I went up to my room. Nobody spoke.

The deep-blue drizzling Salford evening with the street lamps like streaking stars, like dandelion clocks, like a stone smashed through a window.

> *So my life seemed to be*
> *Rain falling unendingly*
> *With thoughts of you*
> *Like lamps piercing monotony,*
> *Radiant, fantastic.*

I think this is the best poem I've written.

I have been at the Ref all day. The door always open. All those shelves of books, that you can take down and read as you please – so many friends just waiting, asking no questions, just talking, and explaining, and telling and sharing . . .

The only thing that isn't peace is the echo. But even that doesn't have to worry you. Sometimes it's like a large excited puppy, bouncing and bounding against the walls, so that I almost laugh.

I've written a whole new act for *Twelfth Night* with a new song. It's for a competition in the school magazine.

★

171

She asked me today where I'd been. And I said 'Kersal Moor'. And she said – she actually said – 'A daughter of mine come back from Kersal Moor with grass in her hair!' It's an extra-ordinary thing for my mother to have said! Even the rhythm is extraordinary – when she always talks in a completely English way. It would be laughable if it weren't so disgusting. I'm so furious, so contemptuous, that that's the only thing she could think, that she would believe at once that's what I was doing!

I thought, He maketh me to lie down in green pastures . . .

I say it out loud, very dramatically. 'A daughter of mine with grass in her hair!' and laugh.

Yet actually, now that I think of it, that is what I was doing.

I walk for miles. I stand outside bookshop windows, I play records in shops. I play my violin in my room, practising the slow movement of *Eine Kleine Nachtmusik*. I go to the Challenge Club and watch *October*. Nat Lerner puts his hand on my knee, a very damp and lifeless hand. He's childish.

My father is doing something I can scarcely believe. I can scarcely say it. He found out I was doing the song – the words and the music – in the magazine competitions, and he said *he* will do it, (*he will do it for me!*) and I will submit it under my name. He says I mustn't send in the one I've written – I must send in his. He is absolutely insisting. I've said I won't do it, I can't do it. But he takes no notice.

He is writing it now. What has come over him? He hasn't had anything to do with me for God knows how long, and now he is taking over what is important to me!

He has gone crazy. He has made me copy it out in my own handwriting.

★

172

When first I saw your face, I resolved to honour and enthrone
  you,
If now I be disdain'd I wish my heart had never known you.
What, I that loved, and you that liked, shall we begin to
  wrangle?
No, no, no! My heart is full, and cannot disentangle.

It is not mine. I did not write it. I am so ashamed.

I have won the prizes for all the things I wrote. I don't want to have anything to do with my father. I don't ever want to see him again.

I went to Simon and Ivy's. I felt so wretched, and angry, but it turned out a good place to go. They leave you alone.

Today I came home from school, and let myself in. He was just inside the door. Waiting for me, I suppose. He said 'Your mother's gone.' The first thing he had said to me, apart from that crazy *Twelfth Night* business, for how many years?

I said 'Thank God' and walked past him. I don't care which of them has gone, so long as they're apart. Now there will be peace.

Incantations

1936

Somehow I have to make some relationship with this man who has not spoken to me for almost the whole of my life, who has simply lived in the same house, and is my father.

He sits in the kitchen and doesn't speak. Except to say he will kill himself. People ring the bell, but he won't answer it, so I have to. He says 'Don't let anybody in', so they stand on the doorstep and they tell me I must do this and that, it is my duty. I am turned to stone. They can't touch me.

Yesterday morning Uncle Larry rang the bell. He had Norman and Leon with him. Why did he bring them? – they're little kids! I suppose it was to 'soften' me. I really despise that.

He told me I should go to my mother; it was my duty. I didn't let him in. I don't know what my father would do if I let anyone in.

The bell keeps ringing. I open the door. I stand on the top step. Someone will tell me my duty. To be with my mother. I suppose they think I'm 'with my father' now. That's a laugh. I say nothing.

A letter has come from my mother. It is from Palestine. I open it. I am cold, not letting myself feel.

She has gone there to look after her father and mother, Bobbie and Zaidie Cohen, who went there to die and be buried near the Mount of Olives. She tells me what I must do, what I must tell my father to do, what my duty to her is. I fold it up again, trying to keep my fingers from trembling, and carefully put it back in the envelope.

The kitchen corner is empty. My father has got dressed.

I've passed all my exams, with distinctions. There's nothing more I can pass now, so they just let me wander about the school, and go to any class I feel like. I go to art and to music. I go to the Ref and stay there all day. I walk through the streets.

Another came today. I open it not too quickly, not too slowly. Carefully.

Today I wrote to her, saying that if she keeps on telling me my duty, I will have to stop writing to her.

I don't know where Mrs Freeman took me yesterday. I have never been out with her before, and I have never seen a place like this. Did my father arrange it? When did he do it?

It was underground, like Aladdin's cave, we went down to it in a lift. Not a dainty lift, but a large one for people with trolleys and huge cardboard boxes. And when we came out of the lift there was miles and miles of perfumes and lipsticks and soaps and powders, all marching along like a holiday, with French names hanging up like banners.

And Tot just walked along with a basket, picking up whatever she wanted, and putting it in her basket. At the end of the miles and miles, she put the basket on a counter. And she didn't pay for anything. She took a card out of her handbag and gave it to the man, and said 'Send it.' It was magical. But she sounded tired, and not interested.

I have never seen anyone take things, anything they fancy! And take it without paying!

As the man took the basket from her, she reached out a hand and picked up something and gave it to me. It was small, and made of gold. A lipstick. I have seen people with lipstick on, and they look like a baby with a jam butty. I think they buy them at Woolworths. But this one, this one that Tot picked out for me – but picked out so lightly as if it was nothing – and smudged it on a slip of paper for me to see, was a creamy peachy orange, like crushed hopscotch. The colour and smell and . . . what do you call it, the *madeness* of it, the way it's creamy and thick and not gritty and so smooth you can feel it without touching it – it is so dear to me.

I want to hold it to my nose as if my nose is listening to it and then lick it, the way a baby does.

I have told my father he must stop saying the things he does about my mother to me. I don't want to hear them. He seems surprised.

Another letter from my mother. She just doesn't listen to what I am saying. I can't write to her any more. I have got to have peace.

Today, I was in Tot's bedroom, and she picked up the valance of her bed to straighten it, and I had that flash again. As if it was someone's frock, and they were going to hit! Hit!

In Tot's house there was Nat Rothman and Lou, Tot's younger brother (no, half-brother) and me. And Tot, of course, but she was somewhere else. Nat and Lou are four or five years older than me. They kept rumpling me, and every now and then one

of them touched my leg under my frock in an absent-minded
way. But most of the time they were chanting Shelley's *Ode to the
West Wind* together. They must have been practising it for days.
In fact I had the feeling that they'd been practising it together the
whole of their lives.

> *O wild West Wind, thou breath of Autumn's being,*
> *Thou from whose unseen presence the leaves dead*
> *Are driven like ghosts from an enchanter fleeing,*
>
> *Yellow, and black, and pale, and hectic red,*
> *Pestilence-stricken multitudes!*

It roared at me, humming, like a storm wind. I didn't know the
words, but they flew inside me and fastened tight like burrs on
a jersey. I can still say them.

> *If I were a dead leaf thou mightest bear;*
> *If I were a swift cloud to fly with thee;*
> *A wave to pant beneath thy power, and share*
>
> *The impulse of thy strength, only less free*
> *Than thou, O uncontrollable!*

They stamped about in time to the words and paced around,
chanting, their voices not dropping at the end of the lines but
lifting like seagulls on the air, watching each other with their
ears.

> *Make me thy lyre ev'n as the forest is:*
> *What if my leaves are falling like its own!*
> *The tumult of thy mighty harmonies*
>
> *Will take from both a deep autumnal tone,*
> *Sweet though in sadness. Be thou, Spirit fierce,*
> *My spirit! Be thou me, impetuous one!*

Drive my dead thoughts over the universe,
Like withered leaves, to quicken a new birth;
And, by the incantation of this verse,
Scatter, as from an unextinguished hearth
Ashes and sparks, my words among mankind!
Be through my lips to unawakened earth

The trumpet of a prophecy! O Wind,
If Winter comes, can Spring be far behind?

It was an orchestra.

They fell on the floor and lay there, silent. Then Nat said that little girls' cunts were very dainty, like tangerine slices. And I had thought so too. And now I thought of the water-ice heaped in an empty tangerine shell that we had at my cousin Minnie's wedding, that was so magical.

I said I was going to be a writer, and as soon as I left school I would get a job on a newspaper. Nat said 'Why? If you want to write, why be a journalist?' And I said 'All writers start as journalists. They have to earn money.' Nat said 'Name one. Just name one decent writer who has started as a journalist. If you want to be a writer, write!' He is studying to be a solicitor. Am I mistaken to think I must start in journalism? We were arguing, when Tot came in. And she said 'The world is so full of unhappy people.' And then she said 'Sol and I are very much in love. I don't care if I'm poor. I was always used to being poor. It doesn't matter, if we love one another.' She had been crying, and she looked very beautiful when she said that, and as if she loved us all very much, and she was *sharing* with me because we were all men and women, and part of the world too. Of course we are, but most grown-ups don't think so.

Who is Sol?

Tread Softly

1936

My father is going to start a practice in London. He has taken a room in Queen Anne Street, off Harley Street (which is a very posh street, I know), and he is going to take the sleeper-train to London every week-end, going up on Friday and coming back on Sunday morning.

On Friday night Fred said I should go up and get ready, and he'd come up in ten minutes. So I went up and washed, and brushed my hair, and put on my clean pyjamas, and put some Yardley's Orchis on the tips of my ears, and plumped up the pillows, and sat up against them, and smoothed out the sheet in front of me. And Fred came in and burst out laughing because I looked like Visiting Time in hospital. Well, I'd never done it before.

He was very gentle and careful, trying so softly to come in, and stroking me and kissing me, and licking my ear till I squealed because it was more than I could bear. And when at last he came inside me, it hurt for a second, one second only, and then some place inside me cried for him, cried to him. And he hovered above me like a bird, dipping into me, dipping, dipping, like a humming-bird, tasting me, flicking me, sipping me, dipping,

dipping, until, at last, I slipped over the top . . . When I opened my eyes, he was lying beside me, propped up on one elbow, watching me. He smiled. He was very pleased. Proud of himself. In the morning we looked at the sheet. Searched. And there was only the tiniest little pinprick.

Fred sits on the edge of the bath and I stand between his legs and he touches my soft dandelion clock, and begins to stroke me, fingering the wet cleft, circling me. I close my eyes and moan, till the earth rocks in my head and the room turns over, and I slide towards the floor. He laughs and holds me up. 'But what is it *like?* What *is* it you feel? Tell me! what is it *like?*'

I can't speak. How can I speak? I manage to mumble. 'I don't know . . .'

'No, tell me.'

'I can't describe it . . . It's a sort of . . . a sort of . . .'

'Somebody said it was a tickle.'

'Yes . . . I suppose it is a sort of . . . a sort of tickle . . .'

'A tickle?' he repeats, disappointed, unbelieving.

Fred has a sort of game he plays that really scares me. My father's train gets into London Road station at seven in the morning. So we know, roughly, what time he will get here. And Fred, deliberately, stays later, and later. Ten to seven . . . Eight minutes to seven . . . Five to seven . . . Seven . . . When I say 'Go! Go!' he laughs at me. One day they will meet on the doorstep.

It must be the Irish in him.

I've had *Daphnis and Chloe* out of the senior school library three times this term already. It's only a thin little book, translated from the Latin, very quick to read, but very lovely – delightful and funny. The way they kiss and hug and even try taking their clothes off and lying down on the ground together, but can't work out what happens next.

★

He leans on his elbow and looks at me, our two bodies stretched out together so very white except for our brown arms, and he strokes me and nibbles me till I am crying out for him, and then he raises himself above me on his arms like a tall white bird hovering, and only his cock darts at me, dips at me, swoops, licks me, flicks me, until I am crying and begging and dripping with pleasure, and then at the last moment slips in to me, and we gasp and sob and sigh, and for a short while he lightly settles on me his cool damp lean body, and we clasp each other, then roll over on our side, one body, one lock.

The right true end of love . . .

I always get a letter from him on Monday. I think he writes as soon as he gets back to his lodgings. Actually I get a letter from him most days. Five or six pages, closely typed.

Or maybe he does it at work in his lunchtime. Do clerks work typewriters? There's always all these typed pages about him and me, which is rather boring. But mixed up with it are poems by Blake and Yeats and Meredith and Donne . . . all sorts of things I don't know.

> *Had I the heaven's embroidered cloths,*
> *Enwrought with golden and with silver light . . .*
> *Tread softly, because you tread on my dreams.*

I put it in my gym-slip pocket, and take it to school.

He undoes my brassière at the back. He takes so long, I can't bear it! I say 'Let *me* do it! Let me!' And it's done in a second.

We undress each other. Our arms get entangled in our eagerness, and we laugh and kiss.

I've discovered the train really gets in hours earlier! It's a sleeper, and you stay in the train as long as you like – you arrange with the attendant what time he'll wake you with a cup of tea. So he could change his mind and walk in any time! And we've no way of knowing!

Fred starts dressing, and I say 'Hurry up! Hurry up!' And he laughs, and deliberately slows down, combs his hair again, picks a bit of cotton off his trousers, considers his tie in the mirror, unties it, and laughs at me in the mirror as he slowly and carefully knots it again, comes over and licks my ear very slowly and caressingly and murmurs Yeats into it – 'I would spread my cloths under your feet . . .' And I beat with my fists on his shoulders and shout 'Go!'

I lie awake, listening to his steps going down the stairs, and the front door's click. Then I watch exactly ten minutes go by on my clock. If something hasn't happened by ten minutes, it must be all right. I once thought five minutes might be enough, but then I thought there was still time for something to happen. So I give it ten. Then I close my eyes and fall fast asleep, till I hear my father moving about in the kitchen.

He wrote bits out of *The Daughters of Albion* in his letter – and said he was surprised I enjoyed it, that I was very young to understand it. So why did he write it!

Fred keeps trying to get me to promise never to shave my armpits. But I won't promise. I do comb my armpits, though. He likes that, and so do I. And I comb my hair down at the bottom. It goes very soft and silky and frothy, like a huge dandelion clock.

When I'm walking along next to him, with all my clothes on, and his hanging arm brushes against my dandelion clock, that I comb each night and morning and that listens for the voice of his hand, my knees give way, and my legs melt like Salvador Dali watches, and I say 'O-o-o-oh' and I blink to try to keep my eyes open. Because what will people on the pavement think if I suddenly close my eyes and slide to the ground? And he looks at me and smiles, like a conspirator.

★

Ah, Sunflower, weary of time,
Who countest the steps of the sun,
Seeking after that sweet golden clime
Where the traveller's journey is done;
Where the youth pined away with desire,
And the pale virgin shrouded in snow
Shall leap from their graves, and aspire
Where my Sunflower wishes to go.

I so love it when Fred tongues my ear. Softly licking. Round and round the inside curls of it like water running into a child's sandpool, gentle at first, then so fierce and strong I cannot stand it, and I cry out and I laugh 'Stop! Stop!'

And when his tongue touches my closed lips till they tingle, nibbling along their line, stroking them apart, and then slipping in . . .

The grave's a fine and private place,
But none, I think, do there embrace.

We were all crowding round Miss Spink's desk, watching the experiment, and I felt a finger touching my neck, just where the hair is very short – stroking it down, coming back, and stroking it down again. I turned round, and it was Sue Morton. I started to say 'Don't do that!', but she said, on top of my words, 'Do you like that?', and started to do it again. 'Does it make you tingle?' she said. 'Does it make you shiver?' She really irritates me.

He dips into me delicately, exquisitely, like an oar into the water, urging us on. His body poised above me, not touching till the very end, when he gently settles on me with Oh, such a sigh.

D.H. Lawrence makes me squirm. He's like a spineless teacher with a squeaky bit of chalk, writing on the blackboard and *demanding* uselessly that you pay attention (while the air is full of love-notes skimming and swooping backwards and forwards disguised as aeroplanes).

I fall about, reading bits of *Lady Chatterley* to Fred. At one bit I am laughing so much I can only manage two or three words at a time before I fall into the pillows, banging them and wailing. It's the silliest, most ludicrous book I've ever read in my life.

Not just silly. Fascist.

Sue Morton keeps getting behind me, and stroking my neck. The first time I think she thought I might like it, but I think now she does it because she likes to see me angry.

Funny the way boys always keep their French letters in old tobacco tins.

Max Brodie has coloured French letters in his tin. All different colours like lollipops. It's a sort of joke, I think, very smart. I think it's disgusting. I'd never sleep with a boy who had *coloured* French letters!

I came through the room, and a girl was sitting in Fred's lap, letting down her long red hair all around him. I despise her. The cheap little stupid little tart. How could he do this!

I am ironing, ironing. And thinking about Fred. I will never speak to him again. Never see him. Press the iron into the board, clench my fist, press, press my anguish into the board! How could he do it?

Nat Frayman is Fred's best friend. They work in the same office. I didn't ask him to help me. It was his idea. He said he would talk to Fred. He says there is a broken brick in the porch and you can put notes in the space. I don't know what to do.

We are back together.

He says she's just a cockteaser . . . But what about . . . ? Oh, *never mind*!

Fred told me that when he was in Little Hayfield last Sunday two girls in thin cotton frocks came up to him, shaking their purses at him. 'Little slags,' he said.

> *Lovely are the curves of the white owl sweeping*
> *Wavy in the dusk, lit by one large star.*
> *Lone on the fir-branch, his rattle-note unvaried,*
> *Brooding o'er the gloom, spins the brown eve-jar.*
> *Darker grows the valley, more and more forgetting,*
> *So were it with me if forgetting could be willed.*
> *Tell the grassy hollow that hides the bubbling well-spring,*
> *Tell it to forget the source that keeps it filled.*

It was in Fred's letter this morning.

Fred's shown me how to hitch rides on long-distance lorries. You have to duck down till you've passed the check-point, or the driver will lose his job, Fred says. But once you're out of sight of the foreman, you can sit up in the cab with the driver, and talk for hours. Do you know what we talk about? Jack London! They worship Jack London, these lorry drivers – he's their hero – they feel he speaks for them! The other person they always talk about is Upton Sinclair. It's wonderful. They know what books are about – about people's lives, about feeding people's anger and giving them hope and making them laugh deep down for joy. Sometimes when we're past the foreman and don't have to be careful, we ride on the back instead, and that's just as exhilarating in a different way. It almost takes off your ears. The next day you find your face is brown as a nut, not from the sun, from the wind. And everyone says 'What have you been doing! Where have you been?'

Sue Morton was doing her usual silly trick today, getting behind me in science experiments. Suddenly she said 'What's that?' I just ignore her now, so at first I didn't say anything. But she said it again, not just curious this time, but, well, put-out. Annoyed, almost. I keep telling Fred not to give me love-bites on the side of my neck, but he just laughs. Generally I can cover them with the collar of my shirt as long as my school tie's pulled up tight: but craning forward to see what's happening lets them show. She really is a pest!

I comb the hair between my legs till it has a life of its own, and makes a frothy hill when my gym-slip is on, and I can feel it without touching it, very live, like sea anemones. Each hair standing up separately, and calling.

Standing up in a crowd at a Hallé concert, with strangers all around me, I can come, without a touch. I just put my thoughts there. Mozart is best. And the Choral. But I can do it with any music. Or even without any.

We made love in a haystack in Matlock! It was so scratchy! I should have kept my clothes on.

We met Ted Willis from London – Fred introduced me. Fred is having a meeting with him. He's secretary of the Labour League of Youth, and pretty well a Y.C.L.'er, Fred says. He talks that London way, but not so whiney.

Fancy Joan Littlewood and Jimmy Miller getting married! We all talked about it. Fancy concentrating all that *spikiness* together, and having double-spiky agitprop children!
    Still, now they can't marry anyone else and spread it around, and that's a good thing.

Actually they're not being so spiky now. *Till the Day I Die* wasn't spiky at all. It spoke out to everybody. It still screams inside me.

When I go up the tramcar stairs on a Saturday or a Sunday, the wind always catches my skirt and blows it right up. And I grab at it, laughing, because my cami-knicks eagerly open between my legs of their own accord.

Why isn't there a proper name for all these parts of me? Vagina and clitoris are medical words that doctors are afraid to say out loud to you in case they're crossed off the register.

And cunt or bush or shag or quin or quim are what people say when they're sipping bitter or lager in the upstairs room before the meeting starts, singing *Bollocky Bill*, and joking in the thick blue Woodbine smoke, and looking at you sideways to see how you're taking it . . .

> *Mother can I go out to swim?*
> *Yes, my darling daughter,*
> *See that the boys don't get at your quim,*
> *Keep it well under the water –*

And you laugh because you're comrades. But they don't have love in them.

Fred said he wanted his mother and his sister to meet me. His mother runs a hotel in Southport and we are going to stay there for a week-end. It's weird! I feel nervous.

Fred's mother is not what I expected at all. I thought someone who ran a hotel would be posh. She is very made-up, like a tart, and her hair looks hard as corrugated iron, and dyed red. And his sister is all scraggy, and my enemy. They are both my enemies.

I thought Fred and I were going to have one room together, but Fred looked quite astonished and as if he wanted to put his hand over my mouth. Even though there were only the two of us together, talking. We are to have separate rooms, and be very polite to each other. It's crazy.

We got tickets for the Ardwick show. I terribly wanted to go. And I wanted to show Fred jazz. He doesn't really know any kind of music.

The stage is in darkness. Slowly a green light comes up. The band, all in black, on the right. Stark white slabs on the other side of the stage. A clarinet crying out, sweet and piercing. A spotlight on the girl singer at the side of the stage. A black girl in a long white dress, very still, singing slowly, drawing a cold slow finger down your spine.

> *I went down to St James's Infirmary,*
> *Saw my baby there,*
> *Stretched out on a long white table,*
> *So cold, so sweet, so fair.*

I can feel Fred's eyes boring into my face. Insisting that I look at him. I am so angry! In the end I turn and look. And he is *smiling*. And expects me to smile back. I hate that! I don't want to be *owned*, and – what's the word – *indulged*!

I brought him here to listen to this terrifyingly brilliant girl singing, not to look at me, in that hateful proud way! I don't think he really wanted to come at all. He was doing me a favour. As if it's a favour to go with someone to something she cares about, when all you care about is *her!* Owning her!

My father says people in Manchester are saying that he isn't looking after his daughter properly, isn't preparing my future, and I am making it very difficult and humiliating for him by refusing to go to University. That perhaps I should think what his position is.

★

I have made a bargain with my father. I won't go to a University, but I will go to a Teacher Training College – but if I don't like it I will leave *within one year.*

I certainly *will* leave. As far as I'm concerned, that's settled already. But it will keep him happy for the moment.

I don't care which college I go to. What does it matter? All I want to do is write.

I'll go to the one that Eva is going to.

We are going to live in London, because of my father's new practice, so I will be able to go back there at week-ends.

Fred is joining the International Brigade.

Yes, Comrade Robson is the man to see. You have to go to King Street in London, and up the bare wooden stairs. He will give you twenty-four hours, to arrange your life.

Twenty-four hours!

And yet, as it turns out, there isn't much to arrange. To say your mother should be notified if you are killed. (Is she more important than me, then? It is like her hotel where we couldn't sleep together.) To ask me again to marry you (and I say no). To give me your *Treasury of English Verse.*

I turn the pages. 'Never seek to tell thy love . . .' 'Under yonder beech tree . . .' 'Shy as the squirrel, and wayward as the swallow . . .' 'Fain would fling the net, and fain have her free.' I look, but I cannot find 'Tread softly because you tread on my dreams.'

On the flyleaf is his name, and the name of his school. And underneath, *Maurice Clift Prize, 1933.* Three years ago. I put it under my pillow.

I stand on the platform at Victoria Station. The train begins to move. Slowly. Then faster, and faster. Now I can see only the back of the train disappearing up the track. Further and further away. Smaller and smaller. And now the train is out of sight. There is nothing to see. I still stand there. Everyone has gone and I am the only person left in Victoria Station, left in the world, and I still stand there. There on the platform. Because I can't move.

Words on a Wire

1936–1937

Fred is in Perpignan. I have had a letter.

Perpignan . . . Shining Popocatepetl . . .

This place is like a dreary elementary school, stagnant and oppressive. It's dust and mould. Nothing to do with children growing. Why don't they ever mention Susan Isaacs? She's our own child psychologist, and she ran that school at Cambridge that was so important, and this college that trains teachers never mentions her.

I sit in my room with its thin partition walls, hearing exactly the words of the girls in the next room on my left, and the words of the two lecturers in the next room on my right, and the loud whisper of the girl somewhere beyond who is confessing a most treasured sin to the lecturer in religion whom she adores. The whisper slithers like a snake under my door . . . like Phoebe's prayers.

I read Fred's letter again.

★

Leila Berg

This college is the most disgusting place. Creepy is the word.

These student rooms are so thinly partitioned that everyone –
literally everyone – can hear every sound you make, every word
you say. Nothing is private.

And everyone is confessing sins. Very humbly, and sickeningly
erotically. It makes me feel ill. What on earth am I doing here?
What does Eva think she is playing at?

You're not allowed to have boys come to see you!

I think they're allowed in if they're in your family. So you
could swear they're your brothers, or your cousins.

But I don't think anybody here ever does. Ever dreams of it.
They're zombies.

Fred is in Albacete. I am reading his letter, in the little train that
crosses the bridge over the Thames, taking me back from
London to college. Always he begs me to marry him. But I
don't want to marry him. I don't want to marry anyone. Even
though I know you're supposed to marry everyone when there's
a war on; that's what girls are for.

But I carry his letter inside me attached to my umbilical cord,
and I take it out and look at it, like that tiny foetus that was my
friend, and I put it back inside me, and the cord tugs and hurts.

Christ, that my love were in my arms,
And I in my bed again!

He says Esmond Romilly is there. Esmond Romilly who started
Out of Bounds.

The people here don't know anything about Spain. They've
never heard of La Passionaria, or of Hunger Marches – Jarrow,
even. I don't think they've even heard of Hitler, or Mussolini.
They're shut up tight in little boxes, and they smell of mothballs
and mould. How can people like this teach children!

★

192

John Cornford's been killed. I managed to get a copy of the *Daily Worker* today – secretly, at the end of a long bus-ride!

There's a photograph of John Cornford in it. He's been killed, in the fight for Madrid . . . It was the day after his birthday. He was just twenty-one . . . And he's doing The Cambridge Clutching Hand. Will anyone else know?

Ralph Fox was killed too.

I am very cold.

Today there was Esmond Romilly's picture. I thought he'd been killed too. But he hasn't been . . .

Only the eight other English people with him have been . . .

Before I came here, I would have thought that if you're shut up in a closed box you're motionless. But now I know that you can move about in a closed box.

Like the little closed boxes in Lewis's when I was a kid, that ran about on overhead wires. And I remember I always thought that there was a message inside that said 'Dead'.

A message came.

Funny, there really *is* a message inside that says 'Dead.'

Why do I cry like this? Night after night after night tearing my inside out, why? I didn't love him, always he asked me to marry him, and always I said no, so why do I cry like this, gasping for breath, and can't stop? Cry and never sleep? And everyone in this place where you hear the slightest sound must be listening night after night. Are they afraid? Or are they gloating?

No one says anything in the morning. They pretend it is private when nothing is private here. Nobody speaks.

There's an Aid-Spain meeting at the Albert Hall. Ellen Wilkinson, Stafford Cripps, and Paul Robeson. I'm going to take them!

★

193

No one is 'allowed' to discuss anything political! No one is 'allowed' to go to political meetings! No one is 'allowed' to go to the Albert Hall! I don't care – I'll fix it somehow!

They'll all have to come with me, when I go back at the weekend. They can all come to my flat for tea.

I mean, we can say that's what they are doing. That will be the reason they're going to London. To have tea at my flat.

They *can't* come to my flat for tea! No one can go anywhere unless that place is on a list previously signed by their parents! This college is an absolute madhouse. Now I've got to get our flat on their lists, with their parents' signature – even though they aren't going there! Even though there's hardly any time!

I've got everyone sorted out – signatures and all – in the nick of time.

There are hundreds of people marching behind banners to the Albert Hall. Trade Union banners, Socialist banners, Communist banners, Co-operative banners, all thumping and rippling in the winter wind. We are standing at the kerbside watching them come in.

I am half-smothered by all the people singing around me, all so much taller. I stand up on the seat, and I sing there. I am so exultant, wild, almost crying.

I don't know the Spanish words. Not even the English words. Because of the Popular Front government, I learned so many songs in French. So I am singing out 'Vous êtes toujours les idoles des masses', while all around me people are singing 'Riego, Riego, we sing of your victory!'

Have you ever seen ten thousand people standing and singing? Like a field of corn dividing in the wind. And every now and then a child sitting on someone's shoulder sends out a personal child's song, like a lark rising up from the corn.

Riego, Riego . . . !

Oh that fits the music!
    And then we sing *The Red Flag.*

I am back at college! Very much so! They really make me sick, these stupid idiots! Margaret has 'confessed' everything – yes, they actually called it 'confessing', whatever dark deed that may refer to – to her Religion lecturer, with whom she's made a disgusting creepy relationship. It must have been most dramatic. 'I confess I have been to the Albert Hall to a public meeting held – may God forgive me – to aid the democratically-elected government of Spain.' And then, one by one, every one of them 'confessed'. A real orgy of 'confession'. It's bizarre. I'd told them over and over again that if they denied everything, nothing could happen. But obviously they like confessing. It gives them a thrill. That hadn't occurred to me.

I'm summoned to the Principal to account for myself, and be expelled.

I packed first. Then I went straight into the Principal's room and said 'Don't bother to expel me. I was leaving anyway,' and walked straight out again, and caught the London train.
    Afterwards I realised, with a slight shock, that she was small, frail, and very frightened-looking, with a wispy grey beard.

I'm writing an article about the disgusting place. I'm putting a big headline on it – 'Do you want teachers trained here to teach your kids?' and I'm writing all the creepy details, everything. I shall send it to *Woman's Outlook*, that Co-op magazine that Annie introduced me to. I should loathe my own children to be warped by people so sickeningly twisted, so ignorant, so masochistic, so ingratiating, so bowing to authority, so loving to confess. I shall tell them everything about how the place is run.

Woman's Outlook has taken that article. I've sent a complimentary copy to the College Library. I hope they'll put it on the reading table, and plenty of people will read it before they realise what they're reading.

I still wake choked with tears. Drowning. When will it stop?

Displaced Aristocracy

1937

I have flatly refused to go to a University.

My father keeps arguing with me. 'Appealing to me'.

I don't want anything to do with intellectuals. They don't *feel* anything. They just talk. They're not real people. Those clods at Training College were bad enough. To follow it up with intellectuals, I'd be crazy.

He says he's not asking me to take a degree any more. He says London University is offering a Diploma course in Practical Journalism, and that will help me do what I want. I've told him that no editor will take on someone who waves a university journalism diploma in front of him – you'd probably get thrown off the premises and spat on – but he won't see it. He keeps saying – appealing for my sympathy – it will look very bad for him.

*

I have made another bargain with my father. It's not ordinary University stuff, so it might be bearable. And it's only two years.

But I've reserved the right to walk out, any time.

This afternoon – I am still trembling with rage – this afternoon I bumped into Uncle Simie at the foot of the escalator at Piccadilly Circus, crowds milling round us. He saw me first. He grabbed my lapel, held on tight, and told me what my duty was towards my mother. He wouldn't let go, gripping my jacket, talking on and on in his thin tight school-teacher voice.

If I'd had a pair of scissors, I'd have taken them out, and clipped off my lapel with his hand clutching it, and gone!

Funny, he reminds me of D.H. Lawrence. A teacher-type. Always telling me what I *should* do. Not that Uncle Simie or a teacher would want you to say 'cunt', like D.H. Lawrence . . . Although I once heard my father say he'd seen Uncle Simie come out of a V.D. clinic. I wonder if that was true . . . Or did he say it to madden my mother?

My father is holding a little girl in his arms. He is singing to her. She has her arms round his neck. Her cheek is pressed against his.

I almost say 'Sorry I intruded.' I go straight into my own room.

She must be one of the refugee children from Berlin or Vienna. He spends all his time with them.

He calls me. He tells me – orders me, curtly – to look after her, while he gets her something to eat.

This is the sort of thing you are supposed to do, so I start to do it. I bend down to pick her up. The kitten dances in through the open door, and the girl stiffens, and screams, *screams*, in my ear, hitting my face. I try to explain to her that he wants to play. I try to show her how to throw the little ball so that the kitten runs after it and away from her. I try to hold on to her with one arm and reach for the ball with the other. But she is kicking and screaming so wildly, I have to put her down. The kitten keeps dancing about all round us, and the little girl is grabbing my legs, and pinching my skin, and getting behind me, still screaming. So in the end, I stop holding on to the girl, and grab the kitten, and take him into the kitchen. I push him into the sink cupboard, winding his stiff tail in after him. I am going to put a bucket in front of the cupboard door so that he can't push it open again, but his tail keeps shooting out and I can't close it. And while I am still trying to do this my father comes rushing back. He flings his arms round the little girl, and shouts at me 'All you care about is the cat! Have you no heart! Can't you hear her crying! All you care about is the cat! You're cruel! You're unnatural!'

I can hardly pull myself up. My body is suddenly very heavy. 'She was frightened of the kitten,' I say. 'I was shutting it away.' I go into my room and close the door.

Later I hear them go out. I open my door and go into the kitchen and make myself some tea.

While I am still drinking it, I hear his key in the lock. I have no time to get into my room. He fiddles about a bit. Then he says, 'I shouldn't have said that. I was upset. I don't like to hear children cry.'

I put down the cup, go back into my room, and close the door again.

Do I have no heart? Because I do not feel anything. I am quite cold. Perhaps I *am* unnatural. Perhaps there is something wrong with me. I just go on doing things, but as if someone else is doing them.

Today I go round to the *Challenge* office, and say can I work as a reporter. To fill in for a few weeks, while I'm waiting to start this course. A chap called Bill Wainwright is the editor. He looks at me, a bit . . . what's the word . . . quizzically . . . but he's taken me on. I don't think there's anyone else in the place.

I think I'll write an article about Mrs Josephine Butler, the suffragist, who organised the prostitutes against V.D. Bill Wainwright says 'Why not?'

I keep reading more and more about her. The article's getting longer and longer.

I *know* it can only be a certain length, so I keep cutting as I write. But it's still long enough now for a fat pamphlet.
    The more I cut, the more unreadable it gets.
    Somehow the more I shorten it, the longer it seems.

I think, the reason is you can't make a piece of writing into a different kind of writing, just by cutting it. A poem's a poem, a short story's a short story, a novel's a novel. They're all their own shapes from the beginning. You don't change one into the other by cutting. But now I'm stuck with a waste-paperbasket full of words, and what I've got left is unreadable.

I don't think we have a kitten any more.

Mick Bennet's girlfriend and Ted Willis' girlfriend are here. They are quite a bit older than me. One of them is very white and hurting-looking. 'D. and C.,' she keeps saying. She sees I don't understand. 'D. and C. is Dilation and Curetage,' she says. 'That's having your womb scraped.' I am very grateful and proud that they have told me. I feel I belong.

Essie, his wife, is Jewish! I mean Paul Robeson's wife! Isn't it amazing! She's not as black as he is – more golden; but she's Jewish. I'm in their flat in Buckingham Street, off the Strand, interviewing him. He's just come back from Spain, and he's going to do *Plant in the Sun* at Unity. He's a *huge* man, like a tree. A chestnut tree, holding out its candles, when he sings. He sang *Lindy-Lou* for me, and he *rocked* it; it was hard not to start dancing.

They clown about, insulting each other for fun – 'Dirty nigger!' 'Filthy yid!' It makes me almost happy.

He has given me a big photograph, and written 'With love – Paul' across the bottom of it.

I must have been fifteen or sixteen when he did *All God's Chillun* with Flora Robson. I was still in Manchester. I wish I'd seen that. I wonder if it played there first. Most things did.

Bill Wainwright says the photograph's not for me. It's for *Challenge*. That's not true. He gave it to me! Of course it will appear in *Challenge* – I know that – but he gave it to me!

Bill Wainwright's taken it for himself. Not even for *Challenge*. I can't get it back. He's the editor. I feel so . . . ashamed.

He cooks meals for me. I really don't want him cooking meals for me. He hovers over me – 'Is it all right?' – 'Should it have a little more salt?' – 'Is it sweet enough?' – 'What do you think of the flavour?' It's a bit late, isn't it, to be showing so much solicitude?

Anyway, it's not that – he wants me to say how clever he is.

I have joined Marylebone Communist Party. I got the address from Party HQ, and walked round this evening to the house.

It's Jack Gaster's house. He's a lawyer, I think. His father's a famous rabbi. Moira, his wife, is the daughter of Robert Lynd, the poet (Sylvia, her sister, is in Paddington branch). Lulu is Jack's sister. And Bill is someone important in N.A.T.S.O.P.A. the printers' union. For some reason, they are all intensely thin, all four of them, and I keep thinking 'Let me have men about me that are fat.' They're a very intellectual lot. They were weighing me up, quietly and politely. I am competent, acceptable. Because I am frozen.

My father cooks again. Breathing down my neck, as I eat. 'Is it all right?' – 'Should it have a little more pepper?' – 'No? . . . A little less?' It's scrambled eggs.

My first party meeting. We stop for a drink downstairs. Someone is singing:

> *Well, hurry before*
> *I break down your door,*
> *Says Bollocky Bill the Sailor.*

Sounds familiar.

This chap Bill pours the beer straight down his throat, without swallowing. A whole pint. I've never seen anyone do that before. It's a trick, I suppose, but impressive. You must pull up something inside, like a sluice-gate. Nobody else looks, so I suppose he's done it often before. Does he taste the beer at all, I wonder?

The branch seems to stretch a very long way. They are talking about the St John's Wood end of it; it's a classy area, I think, but not completely, because there seems to be a rent strike going on there. Jack is very insistent that the tenants should put the rent money aside every week, even though they're not paying it. He is obviously a very intellectual person. In fact, he seems to be ruling this branch with his intellect. Was it in that Van Gogh book, someone said that now Renoir's hands are so arthritic, he paints with his penis?

It's really ironic the way I can walk into London University without question because I've got certificates to show – and I despise it. While what I really want to get into – it's so hard to get going.

This course is unbelievable. I'm not sure whether I'm truly experiencing these extraordinary people, or inventing them.

The trio of young men, for instance, in their elegantly cut suits, carnation in buttonhole, white-tipped cane or rolled umbrella, who always enter together but at an angle, so that you expect them to break into a tapdance . . . are they really there? Are they really students on this course? Or have I walked into a Coward-Cochran review?

They are Honourables, the three natty men at King's. In fact everyone seems to be Honourable this or Lady this or the ex-Duchess of that. The displaced aristocracy of Europe . . . They all look gormless. The three potential tapdancers are the only ones who look competent. But since they never do tapdance, I may be wrong. What are they all doing here, in London University?

Precisely placed in front of the Professor in Modern Literature, within a short arm's length of his billowing and discomforted cravat, a displaced Duchess snores uncompromisingly on the front seat. In his black coat and flamboyant hat, which are surely meant to impress, not to be snored at, he is embarrassed. He raises his voice; but it's useless. She snores in magnificent aristocratic indifference. Two rows behind are the tapdancers.

I didn't know people like this existed. I thought they were dreamt up by P.G. Wodehouse for thirteen-year-olds to read. Why are they sitting in a university lecture theatre?

Margaret and Evelyn are Party members. I see them when I go to Party meetings, but they don't actually talk to me, because I'm so much younger. Evelyn is very elegant and chic. She said to Margaret that she means to sleep with every important Party member. I wanted to laugh, but I have to keep very respectful.

Margaret's feet are beautiful. I don't think I have seen beautiful feet before. In fact, I never realised they could be like that. They look as if they've been sculpted in alabaster – shaped – with care and concentration. She often takes off her shoes, so you look at them.

I suppose because they are so beautiful, you see each of them separately. You don't think of them as a pair like you think of ordinary feet. I once saw a soapstone carving, and it gave you that same feeling that you wanted to curve your palm round it and move it in a slow dance over the slopes and valleys of it.

I'm to run the local Young Communist League, with someone called Alf who's more or less running it now, and be Y.C.L. delegate to the Party branch. There's a local Y.C.L. social on Saturday night that I'll go to.

At King's, the man on my left today, who has a Polish name and is obviously an intellectual, not high society, has been scornfully lecturing me for the past ten minutes – simultaneously with the Professor who is holding forth hopelessly from under his Bohemian hat on Modern English Literature – on methods of birth control, apparently assuming I will find this subject horrifying and shocking and his manner brutal, and will therefore fall passionately in love with him.

What are they all *doing* here?

I am leaning against the wall, not knowing anyone, not really wanting to though I know I must, watching this chap wax the floor – I suppose he's Alf. He seems to do everything – collects money, welcomes people, washes up. Now he is even singing at the mike.

And he is sending the words at me!

> *One day,*
> *When I'm awfully low,*
> *And the world is cold*
> *I will feel a glow*

Just thinking of you,
And the way you look tonight.

Leave me alone!

Mocking. Coaxing. Eyes dancing . . .

Oh but you're lovely,
With your smile so warm,

Leave me alone! I scowl. Grit my teeth.

Knees very slightly bent, rocking a little, he smiles at me. Unperturbed.

There is nothing for me
But to love you

Leave me alone!

I help with the final washing-up, and chair-clearing and rubbish-collecting, scarcely speaking, then walk home by myself, quickly.

I am selling *Challenge* at Marble Arch, standing next to a Blackshirt, who is selling . . . I think, *Action*. I don't look at him.
  One or two people buy from me. Nobody buys from him.
  I am telling myself I must organise *Challenge* sales. Not just do them on my own.

Saturday evening again.
  All through the evening he sings to me.

I can't give you anything but love, baby,
That's the only thing I've plenty of, baby

★

I don't want it! Leave me alone!
  Holding his arms out to me in that laughing way.

Soon we can close down and I can get away.

> *Goodnight my love,*
> *My moment with you now is ending,*

Leave me alone, leave me alone, I tell you!
  He is prising my hands away from my eyes, bending back my
fingers one by one. It hurts.

> *Goodnight my love,*
> *Sleep tight my love . . .*

He throws out his line, the loop tightens round me, and he
laughingly pulls me in.

I am very afraid.

Dreaming of a Song

1937–1938

Another Saturday. Alf sings to me.
    I feel guilty, because I think he used to sing to Helen Mitchell. She is that very lovely girl, Irish, the same sort of dusky bloom on her as Ray Garber had in Manchester. I don't think she is in the Party or the Y.C.L. . . . maybe the Tenants' Defence League. She hasn't said anything to me, but she has that look – that she once had him and now knows she has lost him. She has a sister, Mary, who looks loyal to her. I'm sorry, but it isn't my fault.

He has a cast in his eye. In some odd way, I am half-ashamed of the cast in his eye, I don't know why. Singing to me at the mike again.

> *Goodnight sweetheart*
> *All my prayers are for you,*
> *Goodnight sweetheart,*
> *I'll be watching o'er you.*

★

And the forward thrust of his thighs, slightly swaggering and rocking in that laughing way that makes me limp with longing. Holding out his hands to me.

I have told him about Fred. I have told him, don't try to make me move fast. I am very frightened to feel again.

The French lecturer at King's is exquisitely dressed, and looking for sexual frissons. He looks in dismay at this sodden crowd of vacant débutantes, and snoring ex-Countesses and stern-faced Russian and Polish intellectuals. Dispirited but desperation-driven, he begins to tell a joke. It startles me because it's one of my favourites though I've never heard it told in French before, and before I can stop myself I laugh. And when he gets to the end ('quant à moi, c'est tout au contraire') I am trying so hard to hold myself in that my laughter comes out in spurts like a motorbike, and I have to bend down to examine my shoes. Down there I manage to control myself. I straighten up cautiously, and take a quick look at the others' faces – all blank, uncomprehending, and gormless – and that sets me off again. I am angry with myself. I reckon this man is very vain, and probably uses this joke to find out who he can jump into bed with. But I keep exploding. It's like when you're a kid and secretly trying to let down a squealing balloon that you shouldn't have blown up in the first place, and a squeak spurts out every time you let go. I'll have to get out of this lecture the second it finishes, or he's sure to grab me.

It's sometimes quite a job getting to the back entrance, because there are crowds of people on the stairs as soon as lectures finish – it's like a cinema just before they start the National Anthem – and I'm pushing against the tide. The wretched French lecturer is waiting for me at the bottom of the stairs; and I keep weaving in and out of the mob, ducking under people's arms, and all the time he just stands there in his exquisite saxe-blue jacket, waiting, confidently sure of his appeal. I dodge under someone's arm, and get lost in the crowd.

There are little groups of men on every street corner, selling each other cars. So Bernie says. I thought they were just friends talking. If they aren't standing together on street corners, they're in the Tailors and Garment Workers, he says.

We're going down to the Y.C.L. Warren Street group, Alf and Bernie, and me.

There's a big chap in this group who looks like Ike, huge and towering. No beard, though. Unlike Ike, he hates me on sight – because I'm small, and I'm a girl, and I can toss Marx and Engels and Lenin back to him, and I do, and I'm just as angry as he is about this . . . this confrontation, I suppose you'd call it . . . but more tightly clenched; he's all over the shop.

There are five of them, all members of the Tailors and Garment Workers, all mates, all hating me; but the others are smaller than he is, thank heaven. Alf is very tickled by it all.

At the Party meeting, Evelyn announces she will be known henceforth as Eve. I laugh inside. But she is very serious about it.

There's a Milk Bar near King's. It's open to the street – a bit like Alf's lodgings. I wriggle on to a high stool at the counter – I really need a box to get on to it – and have a Knickerbocker Glory for lunch. You have to start at the top of it, with the cherry, but it's *so high* to reach. A ladder, not a box. Get me a ladder.

This morning, waiting at the bottom of the stairs, the wretched French lecturer actually managed to get hold of my sleeve, but I pulled away, pretending that I hadn't seen him or noticed anything. I should never have laughed at that joke, or shown that I know French that isn't in school textbooks, but he took me by surprise.

★

Every week now the flat is full of Party people, talking, arguing, laughing, and drinking mugs of tea. Jack Miller jokes about it. 'Leila's salons' he says.

My father wanders among them, which I hadn't expected. He says idiotic things about Lenin and Trotsky, I can't make out whether to be sociable, or to be provocative. He tells me the things he said later, as if he's a little boy being daringly cheeky to them.

I am writing a detective story about my father. He is the one who is murdered. Found lying in the library. All the people who are staying, *everyone* has a motive.

It is called *No villain need be* – from Meredith.

> *No villain need be.*
> *Passions spin the plot.*

I have told Jack Miller, but I don't think he thinks it's as funny as I do.

We have a gramophone!

My father has bought some records. Paul Robeson, Galli Curci, Deanna Durbin.

He doesn't know that I talked to Paul Robeson, that he gave me a photograph. Actually I'm ashamed to tell anyone, because I couldn't think how to stop Bill Wainwright from taking it.

Paul Robeson is singing *Old Man River*. I've so often heard people sing it, and they sing it almost jauntily, like a noble, patriotic marching song. But it isn't that at all. It's a bitter song, full of despair. And the lullabies he's singing – *Curlyheaded Babby* and *My Little Black Dove* and *Mammy*, and that other one . . . what's it called? . . .

> *Don't you cry, my honey,*
> *Don't you weep no more . . .*

★

210

My father is always singing them, but missing the sadness. He just cuddles himself.

Galli Curci is singing *Lo, hear the gentle lark*. He talks about the disembodied purity of her voice. He probably read that somewhere.

He loves Deanna Durbin. She is singing the Mozart *Alleluiah*. He does his shaking-his-head-in-amazement act when she holds the top note just before the end. But actually it's not meant to be like that. Elizabeth Schumann sails straight through that top note. Much more exultant, much more triumphant.

I expect someone directed Deanna Durbin to sing it that way.

She *is* delightful, though — honest and unaffected and fresh, with a glorious voice. Fourteen years old.

Every now and then, completely out of the blue, my father will suddenly go off into baby-talk . . . the sort of nonsense sounds people might make to make a baby laugh. He isn't saying it to anyone else. I think he says it to himself, as if he's his own baby. It's irritating.

My father has bought me an 'afternoon dress' from Galerie Lafayette. I've never had an 'afternoon dress' before. I *think* they're for sipping cocktails . . . or is it for afternoon tea? . . . I feel again 'A bit late, isn't it?' I always feel it. I am angry.

We are going to the Winter Garden Theatre to see *Dante the Magician*. We have seats in the stalls, right at the front — I've never sat at the front of a theatre before. I've always been up in the gods.

It was absolutely extraordinary. Dante had his girl assistant bring him two hoops. Just ordinary hoops that you play in the street with. Then she brought him a piece of white paper, and he stretched it over the hoops so that it looked like a barrel. Then she brought a tap, and he stuck it into the white paper, and put the whole lot on the floor. And then she brought him a glass, and he turned on the tap. And golden lager poured out! Everyone gasped.

He turned round and looked at the audience, waving the glass of lager, and picked out – me! Perhaps it was that afternoon dress.

And he asked me to come up on to the stage, and drink it, to show it was real lager. So I did. And the audience clapped like mad. It was crazy. There was absolutely nothing in the barrel.

And after that he filled dozens of glasses, and his girl assistant filled dozens of glasses, and they handed them out all over the audience, dozens and dozens of glasses of inexhaustible lager, from a perfectly empty improvised barrel.

I simply can't get over it. There was nothing there! Truly nothing! My father is angry because he can't work out how Dante did it. He is sitting at the table with a pad of paper, drawing tiny diagrams, and writing out mathematical possibilities in infinitessimal handwriting, and muttering. He takes it as a personal insult. But I am laughing. I feel quite drunk. Drunk with a magic potion.

My father sits down. He opens a little notebook, and sits there, poised, like a stenographer ready to take dictation. He is going to read out a joke from the collection he is making.

The first time he tries one out, I am irritated – I don't want to be part of his life or have him in mine. But I can't help laughing, even though I grudge it.

If I say 'Not terribly funny', he will cross it out, and move on to the next one. I'm . . . I don't know . . . reluctantly charmed.

This time, it's about a rabbi.

The village, in Poland, saves up, and sends him to the Big City, to see what's going on in the world. On the scheduled date, he doesn't return. They wait. And wait. What has happened to him?

Eventually in sorrow they send the warden to search for him.

The warden wanders the city streets, which are unlike anything he has ever seen. He goes to the address they had picked out, a respectable kosher lodging-house. They have never heard of him. He goes to another lodging-house, a little lower in the social scale (no point in going higher). But he is not known there either. He goes to another place, still lower. Not there. He drops lower and lower, till eventually he is tramping up a long flight of crumbling filthy stinking stairs, a room at the top.

He opens the door. His rabbi is in there – in bed with a woman! 'My God!'

He staggers back.

The rabbi raises himself up on one elbow and looks him in the eye. 'It's all right,' he says (the Jewish reassuring sideways handwave), 'I don't eat here.'

Nobody but a Jewish person could know how funny this is. I laugh. Of course I laugh. And go on laughing. Who would have thought my father had so much fun in him!

We have started going to Marx Brothers films. And Micky Mouse cartoons. My father and I.

Swing-doors! We go round and round, several times, tumbling out, staggering and laughing. Into posh restaurants. My father loves taking me to posh restaurants.

We go to see *Animal Crackers*. I get hysterical with laughter. When we come out, he keeps suddenly shouting 'And another hard-boiled egg!' People stare.

We push through swing-doors again. He is still shouting 'And another hard-boiled egg!'

Those old professors in *Horse Feathers*, beards swaying rhythmically, earnestly singing 'Whatever it is, I'm against it!' And Chico, tickling the piano as if it was a baby's chin . . .

213

And that bit in *Duck Soup*, where Groucho talks himself into a rage against the Foreign Ambassador, who has done *nothing* to him at all, so that when he comes in he immediately strikes him across the face and shouts 'This means war!'

And that part with all the animals and the birds! Weak from laughing, I step out on to the pavement, and find myself shouting 'Help is coming!' in my head ('Help is co-o-o-oming!'), and setting hordes of lions, gorillas, eagles, whales, crashing through the jungle, beating back the sky, and cresting the waves, to my rescue. It's glorious!

Oh, Harpo swinging from the chandelier – or hanging in the dressing-gown on the door, with his top hat and dark glasses on . . . And Margaret Dumont, like a ruffled wood-pigeon, shooting out of a cannon on to the mad trapeze act . . . And the orchestra in the band-stand on the lake, playing Wagner at full blast, and drifting out to sea.

I laugh till I am almost sick, and frighten myself.

Odd I'm going out with him after twenty years of silence. And both of us laughing and enjoying it.

Among other things, I'm Y.C.L. Press Officer. I've decided to write letters in the local paper from various invented people. My two favourite characters are a Major, and an old lady. He loves armaments, of course – thinks we should have more of them. And the old lady thinks young people are disgraceful. I weigh in sometimes, as myself, and lecture her in a letter, giggling as I type.

My poor ancient typewriter. The e's are always full of dirt – the e's, and the o's, and the s's. I am always poking them with a bent bit of wire, to stop them looking as if they have little school caps on. The m's and n's too. Oh dear.

Robin Archer has taken to waiting at the front entrance, to take me home! Dear heaven. What is that man doing in the Party, with his suit and umbrella? He pays my fare on buses ignoring my anger, and calls me 'dear little woman'. And he pats me on the head. At least, I *think* he does. I've got so mad at him, I may be imagining it. At intervals he asks me to marry him. He's apparently even spoken to my father! And my father approves of him! Of course he would. He probably thinks – dear heaven – I'll wear an engagement ring on my finger.

I never use the front entrance of King's (except for my Knickerbocker Glory). Alf is always waiting at the back – sometimes Bernie, and Danny, even Cecil occasionally when he gets away from the Dorchester cockroaches – and we leap on to a bus as it moves off along the Embankment, like flying trapeze artistes. The conductor yells at us.

> *He flies through the air with the greatest of ease,*
> *The daring young man on the flying trapeze,*
> *His movements are graceful, all girls he can please;*
> *But my love he's purloin-ed away.*

We sing it.

I stand on our soapbox and talk about Spain, but no one can hear me – not even the usual dog who practically pees on my foot, thinking I am a silent fixture. Some Paddington Y.C.L.'ers and a Party member come along and say I am over the boundary! Go back to Marylebone!

Like the anti-Communists who say 'Go back to Russia!'

In the new Quality Inns, you can have as much coffee as you like, free. But they deliberately make it stronger and stronger each time, so you have to give up eventually.

We walk away, feeling a bit strange. At least, I do. Not quite fitting my body. Like tracing paper that's slipped a bit.

How do you know whether to say 'plastic' or 'plahstic' . . . or 'elastic' or 'elahstic'? Or 'lurry' or 'lorry' . . . or 'wurry' or 'worry' . . . or 'woory'?

How do you know? Who is in charge?

They laugh at me.

The trouble with my newspaper campaigns is, I never get a discussion going, which is what I'm trying to do. I mean, the only discussions I get going are among my invented characters and me. No one else is interested.

Oh, those Soviet Sportsgirls on the pages of *Challenge*! Bent back like bows, their breasts straining against their Aertex blouses, their nipples like the thrusting tips of arrows – Twang! and they speed off into the sunrise! We laugh at them.

> *Il va vers le soleil levant,*
> *Nôtre pays.*

Didn't Shostakovitch write the music for that? Or am I thinking of the song in *Road to Life*? – I always mix them up.

Actually they're rather like the girls in *Happy Mag* or *Sunny Mag*, or the railway posters, sitting on a rock and waving. Skegness! Southend-on-Sea!

I am still selling *Challenge* at Marble Arch corner, next to that Blackshirt.

Today I take the unsold ones home, and open one up – what d'you know? Masses of Soviet Sportsgirls!

There's a big photograph of all the girls elected to the new Soviet Parliament. All of them are seventeen years old – well, one or two are as old as nineteen, even – all tractor-drivers, or else treasured Stakhonovites – all doing their twentieth parachute jump or flying aeroplanes in their spare time! And they look so lovely. Golden-haired too, probably.

★

We go to the Met in the Edgware Road sometimes, Alf, Bernie and me, sometimes Cecil too, sometimes only the two of us.

Max Miller! He doesn't even have to open his mouth! He doesn't even have to come on to the stage! He just sidles on to the wings, and stands there, until someone in the audience notices him, and a ripple of laughter spurts up and spreads like a forest fire until everyone is weak with laughter! And he is doing nothing! Just standing at the side, gazing at us amiably! Compassionately, even. I don't know who's funnier, Max Miller or Max Wall. And both so utterly different. Max Miller so confiding, wheedling; and Max Wall, totally unsexual, aloof, intellectual, anguished, solitary, wildly demented. Whichever of them it is, I bang up and down on my seat, crying 'I can't bear it! I can't bear it!' We come out limp and exhausted, staggering about the pavement, blind with tears, and bumping into Snowy who is still selling papers and looks at us pityingly.

Stardust. Such a sweetly meandering tune, so personal and private that you seem to be eavesdropping. Alf plays it on his mouth-organ.

> *Sometimes I wonder why I spend these lonely nights*
> *Dreaming of a song . . .*

Harmonica, says Cecil, being Dorchester.

Larry Adler still calls it a mouth-organ.

Last night they took me to All-in Wrestling. I've never been before. They said it was all set up, and just a good laugh, a sort of pantomime act. Not like real wrestling which is an art. Everyone was shouting 'Kill him! Kill him!' and the wrestlers were making the most contorted faces as if they were in agony, and everyone howling with laughter. (I suppose they really *are* pretending?)

I've never seen anyone do that before – hold their nose with one hand, and pull an imaginary lavatory chain with the other, like Alf does. Must be London.

Bernie shows me how to pick a lock with a piece of celluloid, or even an old postcard. Cecil somehow manages to be very supercilious all the time this is going on. Not that he wouldn't do it, but that he would do it in a much more Dorchester way. It keeps making me think of that story in Bennet Cerf's book (and in my father's notebook) 'That is all very well for Lyon's Cornerhouse. But at the Savoy we use a warmed soup ladle' – and I keep snorting with laughter.

I get a letter signed by G.B. Harrison, my tutor, this morning – polite but rather terse, asking me – telling me – to call in and see him.

I turn up at G.B. Harrison's rooms. On time. I think I'd better.
    Before he can speak I say haughtily, but fast, to get it in first, 'I know I'm often late for lectures, and sometimes don't come at all, and I know I haven't joined any of the students' activities, but I'm perfectly up-to-date with my work, or I can at least be up-to-date with my work if I need to be, and I really don't see any reason – ' He cuts short my indignation by saying – laughing! – 'My dear young lady, I am not complaining about you at all!'
    I am so surprised, I lose my place in what I am saying. He says 'I simply wondered if you intend to continue this course.' So I start off again more haughtily than ever, but he picks up a newspaper and waves it in my face, to make me cool down and stop again.
    Then he actually tells me that most people who come on this course only stay until the *Tatler* prints their picture ('Lady Priscilla who is studying journalism at London University with her favourite foxhounds') – then they're never seen again. So at a certain stage he always asks each student would they oblige him by saying if they intend to sit for the University Diploma.

I am thrown so completely off balance by this mad story, am so won over to sympathy, that I say yes, I do. Anyway, I've made an agreement with my father. He says he is pleased, because the stuff I turn in about the other students and the lecturers is very naughty and malicious, but it makes him laugh, and he can do with something to laugh at.

Kissing Fever

1938

Someone called Tommy has arrived. He says he was a friend of Fred's, and that Fred gave him my address. He tells me it was Franco's Moors who killed Fred. They are professional killers, of course. I mustn't let myself think about it. He describes their knives in a sort of gently charmingly calculating way. I think he tells me this to make me break down so that then he can comfort me and kiss me.

He says scarlet fever is raging in Madrid, and hundreds of people are dying. He's not a political person at all. I should think he's never read a book in his life. Just a young quite good-looking boy. What was he doing in Spain?

He seems to think because he knew Fred he can make love to me. In the end, I let him kiss me, just once. That's all.

I was in the middle of talking to Alf – I mean that literally. I was in the middle of a sentence – when it seems I just fell to the floor.

Alf and I were standing next to each other in the middle of the room, talking, and I began to say something in a perfectly normal way, not feeling anything at all wrong, and it seems I never reached the end of the sentence.

I don't remember anything until just for a moment I found myself sliding off a stretcher in the tiny lift that holds only two people. The ambulance men must have strapped me on to it, and tipped it up on its end, vertically, to get it into the lift. I came to for a second, when I slid down and they grabbed at me, and then I floated off again.

I came to again in the ambulance, speeding through London, bumping up and down, bell clanging. Just for a second, seeing the street through the windows, then out again.

Three days later they told me, I came to properly. In the London Fever Hospital, East End.

I am so tired. I feel drained, like a teapot emptied of tea, and turned on its side on the slopstone to dry. Slopstone. That's Lancashire. What do they call it here?

The room is full of boys in spotless white gowns milling about, making demands of me. I hear them as if they are in the next room. Maybe they are angels. There's Maurice Carpenter, who calls himself Miles now, after the Chartist, who keeps saying he's got involved with some girl and that it's all my fault because I wasn't there, and what am I going to do about it, and he's drearily serious. And there's Fred Skipton who says he's fixed up with a new girl because she reminds him so much of me (does he tell *her* that?). And they both have immaculate gowns on. And there's Bernie in his haircut-and-shave suit, with a snow-white gown over it, and Danny White in his errand-boy rig-out with a snow-white gown on top, and Cecil with his commi-waiter-in-the-Dorchester-kitchens suit with a snow-white gown on top. And there's Alf in his one shirt with both sleeves in trailing tatters up to the shoulder, and a snow-white gown on top. How did they all get in? Did they all say they were my brothers? What is the matron of this mad hospital thinking of? I close my eyes again, and they mill around. I wish they would go away. I am so tired. Except for Alf. I wish he would sit beside me, and hold my hand, and not say a word.

Tommy was a carrier. He brought me Spanish scarlet fever. Nothing wrong with him, of course. That seems right. It was just the impression I'd formed of him.

The head porter is furious with me. The whole building has been fumigated in the weeks I've been away – especially the lift. And it hasn't done him any good either that someone has been carried out – publicly, in broad daylight – on a stretcher.

And now this! Glandular fever *and* Spanish scarlet fever so close together is a bit thick. Not that this glandular fever is anything very much, but it seems it's something you only find in a text-book (which pleases my father no end) – like the dinosaurs. Nobody has it now, except me. It's called, colloquially, (my father says, quoting but not acknowledging his textbook) The Kissing Disease. Well, well.

Alf and I are poster-sticking again. Slapping them up, sloshing them, flick, flick, smoothing them down. And striding merrily away whistling, bucket slurping, shoes splashed, past the cops who stand with their backs to the Edgware Road palings. It's like Flanagan and Allen, we have the timings and the moves so perfected. We only just stop ourselves laughing out loud.

Alf, Bernie and Danny arrive at the door. Something is tickling them. I ask what the joke is, and they say the head porter has made them use the service lift at the back of the building. I am absolutely furious. I rush out of the flat, leaving the front door wide open, straight down to the reception hall where the head porter is talking ingratiatingly to a middle-aged lady all furs and pearls, stand on my toes, and give him a whacking slap across the face. 'Don't you dare be so insolent to my friends again!' I shout at him, and walk back, fast, trembling with rage.

Alf and the others are still standing at the open door, very startled. Danny tries to make me laugh at it. I am startled too. When I have stopped trembling, I try to think how I had managed to reach the head porter's face. Had I unconsciously stood on a box or something?

The head porter has told my father I am lowering the value of the flats. I said 'Lowering the value of the flats! – when everyone knows he lets empty ones out by the night to high-class tarts!' My father was a bit shaken. He thinks Lester Court is very posh.

Sunday mornings at Speakers' Corner, crowds milling over the road, people threading their way from pavement to pavement, sauntering across as they call to friends, a huge Sunday morning club that takes over the top of Park Lane in a weekly celebration.

And the speakers, all old mates too, with their audience of friends who encourage and heckle, and applaud and boo, and chorus together the speeches that everyone knows by heart.

But some are very serious, good socialist speakers, or free-thinkers; lots of people get their education here. I do, like I did from the theatre and the cinema and concerts and bookshops and Manchester Ref – all great celebrating places, much better than schools.

Yesterday Tony, one of the barrowboys, was putting strawberries into a bag for a woman, and she was fumbling in her purse for the right money, and the policeman came up and said 'Move on!' and she grabbed at the strawberries, and Tony tried to grab at the money, and the policeman moved in and started to man-handle him. He had to pick up the handles of the barrow and trot round the corner with it (us scuttling along with him) and set it down again there. They're always moving them on.

They all know each other here, and I think they accept it's a sort of game that has to be played . . . But suppose a stranger, who isn't part of all this, comes up to buy, and when he's going to pay a policeman says 'Move on!'

It's just like *Crainquebille*, that Anatole France story we did in the Junior Sixth . . . still going on now, here in London. It makes me furious.

Alf is ill. He lives in Warren Street. His landlady's Italian. His one room stands open to the sky, like the book-caves of Shudehill, not a room but a shelter for animals. He pays ten bob a week rent, and the Italian woman – the mother – who lets me in, is fond of him, and is glad I have come to see him. There is a bed here, and a sort of chest. He lies, with rags for covering, in a fever.

I have used the last money I have to buy bunches of daffodils, and I come up to his bed with them all in my arms. He looks so white and thin. He opens his eyes, looks at me, and laughs.

For days I have thought with anguish how I bought daffodils when he needed good food – milk or eggs – and how he laughed at me and kissed me.

I suppose Italians don't know that a room that stands open to the sky is strange, because in the south of Italy there are rooms like that cut into the hillside.

Alf is better. He's got a temporary job at Lord's, picking up balls, and collecting tickets. Bernie goes along too, sometimes. It means a bit of money – and they can watch the cricket too – and Alf is getting so brown. I wouldn't mind going myself, but they don't take on girls.

His shirt – shirt? It's rags! – is always very white and clean, as if it had been hung over brambles all day and night.

I went to a big sing-along and saw Jimmy Miller – only he calls himself Ewan McColl now! Ewan McColl! I can't believe it! Now that really is romantic! *Ewan McColl*! Even better than Miles Carpenter.

*

Funny how being in love makes you do daft things. Especially boys. Alf pinched a parked car yesterday evening, and raced it for miles over London, and just left it somewhere, he doesn't even know where, and walked all the way back.

Bernie told me. He just says he was so happy.

I was really frightened. 'Why did you do such a mad thing!' I said. 'Are the police after you now?' And he laughed, and kissed me.

We were walking – walking! that sounds so ploddy! We were dancing, skipping, *bouncing* along the Strand – and Alf bought me a bunch of violets from a flower-seller, and fastened them into my jacket. They were so brilliantly-glowing, so drenched with scent and drenched with colour. And we looked in the window of the Pet Shop – that posh, expensive pet-shop in the Strand – and there were five lovely puppies in an exquisite basket, most of them drowsing or yawning, one of them yapping excitedly, and we went in and said we'd like to buy a puppy. And she looked at us as if she didn't believe us but she couldn't say so. And she lifted out the noisy squirming one and put him in my arms. And the violets, the smell of them and the sight of them, made him even wilder, drove him into an uncontrollable ecstasy, and in a flash he had gobbled up the whole bunch! The lady was struck motionless and speechless. I handed him back to her, remembering to say as I did when a child, 'I'm sorry, he's not exactly what I was looking for' (but my voice trembled), and we fell out of the shop and exploded with laughter, and tottered about in the street, moaning.

The thing that makes the head porter maddest of all is when I slide off the back of a lorry as it passes Lester Court, shout good-bye to Alf, and walk past him and straight into the residents' lift, swinging a paste bucket. He is invariably talking to a very smart lady or gentleman, and goes pop-eyed and purple.

I went into the rubber-shop this morning to get a cervical cap. I read about them in Norman Haire's book. It's actually Elia's book.

He brought it back from Cambridge, but he is letting me keep it.

Really I want to get a Dutch cap, but you have to be measured for those by a doctor, and they won't do it unless you're married. I don't want to go to Woolworths and get a cheap wedding-ring, or even a curtain ring, like some people do. I hate that sort of pretending. I'd sooner manage with a cervical cap, plus jelly and French letters.

There was an enema draped like a dead Indian Rope Trick in the window, and a cold damp smell inside as if the floor had just been mopped but it hadn't, and a man in a dark suit to serve, and another man in a dark suit to keep him company, and they were both sitting on chairs behind the counter, and they both stopped talking when I came in and stared at me expressionlessly. It's not like a shop at all, really. Shops are happy places, busy places. This is more like a funeral parlour. In fact, I'm not sure there wasn't one of those white funeral urns in the window with the dead Indian Rope Trick.

Boys get their French letters from lively places like the barber's. A barber's is like a men's club. French letters, and bets, and selling cars, and bagels and cream cheese, and short back and sides, and a shave. I know – Bernie tells me. Why is it so dreary for girls when they're the other half of it?

Last night we were in Regent's Park, making love on one of those benches in the Inner Circle, and we were just on the brink when we suddenly realised we were getting locked in. We fastened our clothes and ran. But we were too late. We had to climb out over the gate in the pitch dark. It is crazy that Alf never manages to get inside me.

And at Lester Court, there we are on the carpet, and someone always rings the bell. And we drag our clothes together, and fling open the casement window and scissor it to and fro to clear the air. And part of my inside aches for what it was promised and didn't have.

★

It's a bit like Fred pushing it to the limit and almost meeting my father on the doorstep . . . Me with a copy of *Lilliput*, reading one of my favourite Zozchenko stories – in front of the English lecturer – about the sickeningly bourgeois girl who leaves her teethmarks in the cream bun, and trying not to snort with laughter. Then I read a Thurber one, or some more Zozchenko (I come supplied). And he just goes on, preening and polishing himself. He really doesn't need us.

In the papers Haldane is saying that the fascists are rehearsing in Spain their war against England.

The wooden stairs.
 Comrade Robson.
 Twenty-four hours.
 What does he own but a birth certificate and a harmonica?

Victoria Station. My feet, turned towards the retreating train, grow through the soles of my shoes and the stone of the platform and into the earth below, and take root. I still stand on the platform, not seeing anything.

Calais
Paris
Perpignan
Albacete

Someone just back from Spain says they're smoking grape leaves and walnut leaves now. I send Alf two twenty-packs of Players.

A letter! Someone has nicked his harmonica. Yes, yes, I rush to get him a new one. I am so happy to get him something he has asked for. I scrape together everything I can, and get him such a proud, gleaming one.

Have I been silly? Is this what he wants? Perhaps I should have

bought him a very ordinary simple mouth-organ? After all . . .
Stardust . . . it doesn't need something so gleaming . . . so
ostentatious . . .

Have I been silly? Was it wrong to have bought it?

Fred Skipton has come back from Spain. He wasn't there very
long. He helps me with the washing-up.

I say to him curiously, 'What did you learn in Spain?' (This is
the sort of thing we ask in the Party.)

He thinks for a moment, then says 'I learned to do this.' And
he takes a pile of three or four plates, dries the top one and the
bottom one, slips the top one over to the bottom and dries the
top and bottom again – like we all do. 'You don't have to dry
each one separately,' he explains.

A ragged wallet has come.

So stiff. The blood has dried now.

Inside a tattered birth certificate.

All he possessed.

I am down as next of kin. And in receipt of all his posses-
sions.

Did he get the mouth-organ in time? They die so fast in
Spain.

I shouldn't have spent the whole morning choosing the best.
Perhaps it would have caught an earlier post and got there
sooner, and he could have played it longer.

Gateshead . . .

It says in his birth certificate he was born in Gateshead . . .

Yes . . . I remember . . . He told me . . .

I take Eugene Lyon's book off the shelf, and find Vanzetti's last
words, before they executed him. 'If it had not been for this
thing, I might have lived out my life talking at street corners to

scorning men. I might have died unmarked, unknown, a failure. Now I am not a failure . . .'

It's true. He was so long on the dole.

I sit on top of the bus, at the front, and want to smash my fist through the glass. To feel the blood, real blood, trickling down. The real raw pain.

I hold fast and don't do it.

Waiting in the Dark

1938–1939

I wait in the dark. The light is off. It switches off automatically. When it goes on again, someone has come in.

Feet chug up the stairs. Turn off down a corridor. The light clicks off again.

I lean against the wall. I always lean against the wall. Hands in my coat pockets. This damp and cold place!

The light comes on. Feet chug up the stairs, to the end of the first flight. Turn off down a corridor. Light goes off again.

I lay my hand on the hinge of the door in the dark. I wait. I move my hand over the hinge of the door as you might over the thigh of your lover. But without feeling.

The light comes on again. Feet chug up the stairs. Turn off down the corridor. Light goes off again.

Sometimes I wait a long time. I never arrange anything. I just come round. The hinge of the door is a friend.

The light comes on. Feet chug up the first flight. Light goes off. Light comes on again. Feet chug up the second flight. Light goes off. Light comes on again. Feet chug up the third flight.

I push myself off the hinge, off the wall, and stand up straight.

He sees me. 'Hello,' he says. 'Been waiting long?' I shake my head. I don't speak. I don't speak much now.

We go in. He puts his *Humanité* on the little table. I take off my clothes.

His body is long and thin. He doesn't lie on me. Hovers above me, like Fred. Sometimes he licks my cunt. He asks me to lick him. I should feel it. I feel nothing. But I am glad, without feeling, to be with him.

Sometimes Bill puts records on. He brings them back from Paris. Maurice Chevalier singing *Ma Pomme*. And Josephine Baker. Backerrr.

Afterwards, we walk to Bertorelli's. Bill always gets a bottle of red wine. I have half a glass. He talks to me, quite matter-of-factly. But I don't speak.

Once his aunt was in the flat. I suppose she is quite old. After all, he is old enough to be my father. 'Willy, Willy,' she cried out in reproach, seeing me following him into the flat, 'Elle n'est qu'une enfant'. 'Elle est ma copine,' he said. 'Willy,' she began again, worried for me. But he said 'Tais-toi. Elle comprend français,' and she shut up. I said nothing.

Night after night leaning against the wall.

In the corridor the dark is kind. Gentle-handed.

Often he puts that barrel-organ song on . . . *Le Temps des Cerises*.

> *Quand nous chanterons, le temps des cerises,*
> *Et gais rossignols et merles moqueurs*
> *Seront tous en fêtes.*
> *Les belles auront la folie en tête*
> *Et les amoureux le soleil au coeur*

> *Quand nous chanterons, le temps des cerises,*
> *Sifflera bien mieux le merle moqueur.*

It goes round and round, a rickety tinny mindless tune.

> *Cerises d'amour, en robes pareilles,*
> *Tombant sous les feuilles en gouttes de sang . . .*

I hear it as if it is on a street corner the other side of this building.

He once told me it was a song of the French Revolution.

In Bertorelli's, Bill is saying the unemployed miners have been carrying a coffin all over London, and gone into the Ritz for tea. His voice is very far away, like a train whistling in the night, fading.

I am pregnant.

I am angry.
    For the first time for a very long while, I am beginning to feel something.

I have been careless. Yes, I really mean careless. I had stopped caring. You have to care with these cervical caps. Even though Bill's using French letters; he always uses one.
    But I hate him for doing this to me. For making me dependent. I will pay him half what it costs, because I am angry with him, because I had a share of responsibility, and because I am beginning to care. I am angry, and I will pay my share.

This woman friend of Bill's is kind and reassuring. She says the doctor is an anti-Nazi refugee – a Jewish doctor, an experienced gynaecologist. The British Medical Association won't let them practise here. So they have to do whatever they can to keep alive, even if it's illegal. She says I should take a packet of sanitary

towels and a sanitary belt with me, and enough for a taxi fare.
And the money.

It is a very bare place.

I lie down, and the doctor pushes the instrument up me, and
twists it. For a second, two seconds, it is excruciatingly painful.
But it is over.

The doctor was angry with me. Because he is illegal. He didn't
want to look at me. His eyes were hurt and angry. He is a good
man, a skilled man.

I go home in the taxi, three towels fastened to me.

I let myself in. My father is there. I say I have a bit of a
headache, and close my door, and lie down on the bed. He is
a doctor, and is quite unaware that his daughter is having an
abortion.

I am paying Bill back fifteen pounds. That's half. I give him two
pounds every fortnight. He is angry. He doesn't want any money
from me. I am glad he is angry. I just put down the money, and
say nothing.

Teddy Cross's mother must have been crying for a long time.
Moira Lynd talks to her in a very cool way as if she has everything under her control, and as if Teddy's mother is being
unreasonable and bad-mannered to mind that Teddy has been
taken away from her and killed. I am ashamed to be here on the
doorstep with her. The Party wanted me to come because I was
supposed to be Teddy's girl. I wasn't at all; I just let him kiss me
because he was going to Spain, and I lent myself to him for that
very short time before he left, just to make him happy. It can't be
right to talk to people in a superior way because they're crying
and we aren't.

I am reading a terrible, terrifying, short story.

Was there really a disaster like this? A penny-pinching building site in America? Men pinned upright and buried in pouring concrete?

God! His workmates, headless, armless, around him. And he tries to bite an air-hole for himself, but his teeth break off, and can't even fall out of his mouth, but are locked back into the concrete. God!

I have finished it, but I sit still for a long time, my eyes closed, rubbing my forehead with two fingers, up and down . . . Christ in Concrete . . . John dos Passos . . . God!

Haldane takes me to the Zoo. It is Sunday morning, and it's closed to the public, but he is a Fellow of the Royal Society. We go inside cages. We visit Bill the puma, who is his great friend, he says, but I don't feel is mine. Not with those eyes. But the python! Haldane winds it round and round me, and it feels warm and friendly and dry and sane and humorous, somehow. When I had thought it would be cold and slimy, because that is what people tell you – or lead you to believe in some insidious way.

Haldane says we must have deep bomb-proof shelters.

There's a big piece by Haldane in the *News Chronicle*, ending furiously 'If London is raided, it is possible that some of the people responsible for the chaos – and some who are innocent – will be hanged on lamp-posts.'

The International Brigade has come home. All that is left of it.

Haldane invites me to his wife's birthday party. 'But she doesn't know me!' I say.
  'It doesn't matter. She'll be pleased you've come.'

I'm very doubtful. Still, I go.

There are literally hundreds of people in this huge house, all the sort of people I don't know. A queue of people waits to greet her. I shake hands with her, feeling like a little girl.

'How kind of you to come,' she says.

Haldane pulls me out into the huge dark garden, and immediately unzips his trousers and pulls my hand inside. I like Haldane, and if this is what he wants I don't mind doing it for him – anyway, I wouldn't want that hulking weight on top of me, and I shouldn't think he knows how to keep it off you. But I don't want to do it at his wife's birthday party.

Reg's body is tanned gold, smooth as an apple. Ben's body is a thick mat of golden red hairs that glint in the sun. Dennis is white with dark damp curls. He is Dennis now, no longer David.

Haldane has announced he is prepared to sit in a surface shelter and have explosives let off all around him, nearer and nearer, while people record what happens. He says the Government has got to provide deep shelters.

I go to see Bette Davis in *Dark Victory*.

That shot in the garden when she says how dark it is getting – and yet she can still feel the sun shining on her arm! And she remembers what the brain surgeon said, that that is how the end will be . . . And she goes back into the house, to die.

We lie on the grass by the Serpentine and make love. Legs of people passing in the buttercups, seen against the sky. Armpits that smell lovingly of toast (Makes me think 'Stands the church clock at ten to three?' and I laugh). And the grass, so cool, that criss-crosses your body in trellis pattern. Everyone is on the dole.

I choose them. 'Would you like to come into my bed?' I turn back the sheets for them. They are so happy to have me. It is so good when people are happy to have you. To be so welcome . . . a gift.

Now Reg, who was always so debonairly immaculate, Reg too has a white shirt that hangs in rags. Rags will be absolutely normal dress soon. And always white, such brilliant white, through all the lying in the sun by the Serpentine after signing on for the dole.

It seems darker, doesn't it . . . doesn't it? Yet I can still feel the sun shining on my arm . . .

Haldane says the deep tube shelters could be used.

I have had ten offers of marriage in as many weeks. How conventional and idiotic the Communist Party is. I sleep with a boy, and immediately he asks me to marry him. Supposing I said yes. Where would we be?

Haldane has had himself sealed up in an underground room, to test out what happened to the ninety people who died in the submarine disaster.

They say he is still alive after fifteen hours of it.

I didn't bother to collect my diploma, so they've sent it on to me. And a letter from G.B. Harrison to say my English Literature paper was the best they'd had for many many years.

I am on holiday with Helen, from the University. (At last I'm having a holiday at a friend's house in the country like people do in school stories!) They live in buttercups-and-daisies country, yellow and white in the grass, with bellowing cows mad-drunk on apples, like Mr Butterworth said all those years ago. We walk through the little lanes picking wild flowers. On the way back, Helen's mother crouches down among the trees and pees. I feel so happy for her, that she does such unacademic things.

★

I keep looking at my arm, then up at the sky.

When we get back to the house, her father has his finger on his lips, pointing to the wireless.

Germany has invaded Poland.

We stare at each other. I say 'I must go back to London. At once.'

They look at me gravely, with respect. I don't know why I feel I must go back, but I do, as if the war can't start without me, as if I am of vital importance.

And they must agree, for they come at once and help me pack, in that same gentle grave way (they are Christian Pacifists . . . Quakers perhaps) and wave me off at the tiny country station. Will she have to pee in the bushes on the way back? Helen says she can never last out both ways.

Saturday. I keep turning on the wireless, but there is nothing. Nothing is happening. We are in No Man's Land, holding our breath.

Sunday. The wireless. Chamberlain says he has asked Hitler to stop (at long last, when he has cheerfully watched him invade country after country) but Hitler won't. Chamberlain, his friend, who has encouraged him all along, now asks him politely to stop! What a farce! So now we are at war. In Trafalgar Square Bernie is there, and David who sometimes calls himself David and sometimes Dennis, and Cecil with his scornful intellectual look as if he knows everything we don't.

We begin to talk in an uneasy, nervous, ragged sort of way. And suddenly – a terrible sound! It freezes our words in mid-air. Surely it has been invented by an enemy, that unearthly wailing that turns your limbs to water before a bomb has been dropped? It moans on and on, up and down, swooping, scooping, sickeningly. The first air-raid siren.

We stare at each other. Then look away, afraid to meet each

other's eyes. No one knows what to do. Should we laugh it off? Should we joke about it? Say something biting and clever? Pretend we haven't heard it? Make a brief political statement? Be afraid?

At last it has stopped.

Our Sunday morning – all our Sunday mornings – have crumbled away. And one by one, we fall silent, we disperse, we disengage from each other, not wanting company (we have never done that before). Something new is beginning, and we fumble because we don't know what it is. I look for a 113 bus, while for some reason pretending not to.

That monstrous howling still hangs in mid-air like a torn limp rag on a tree after a storm.

On the bus everyone stares straight ahead, showing nothing, English-wise.

Some Background Information

Shabbos, the Sabbath, which is Saturday the seventh day, starts on Friday evening at sunset, when the mother lights the candles.

Perony, loose feather-bed.

Frum, religious.

Bobbie, Granny.

Zaidie, Grandad.

Shool, synagogue. Men pray in the main room, women in the upstairs gallery.

Ingberlech, sweetmeat, made of carrots and ginger.

Lockshen, long thin noodles.

Cheder, Hebrew and religious class – for boys.

Med, drink made from hops and honey.

Taiglech, sweetmeat made from dough cut into tiny chunks and soaked in honey or syrup.

Chazan, trained singer (cantor) who leads the service in shool.

Purim, a festival, that celebrates the story of Queen Esther of Persia, who defeated a conspiracy against the Jews.

Passover (Pesach), a festival, that celebrates the march of the Jewish slaves out of Egypt. Cupboards are scrubbed out, crockery and cutlery are changed to the special ones for Passover.

Bubbele, darling.

Boychik, darling boy.

Bar mitzvah, celebration for a boy's thirteenth birthday, announcing that he is now an adult.

Succa, an improvised 'dwelling' to commemorate the time the Jewish people were wandering, homeless.

Orthodox Jewish women cut off their hair, when they marry, and wear a plain wig instead.

Men, when praying, strap little cases holding the word of God to their heads and arms in literal obedience to the Bible: 'and these words which I speak unto you this day shall be upon thine arms, and they shall be as frontlets between thine eyes . . .'